Every Yes

How Radical Obedience Unlocks Your Purpose

JEN MATTHEWS

EVERY YES

Copyright © 2025 Jen Matthews
All rights reserved.

ISBN:
979-8-9993061-3-5

Unless otherwise indicated, all Scripture quotations are taken from the Holy Bible, New Living Translation, copyright © 1996, 2004, 2015 by Tyndale House Foundation. Used by permission of Tyndale House Publishers, Carol Stream, Illinois 60188. All rights reserved.

Scripture quotations marked MSG are taken from The Message, copyright © 1993, 2002, 2018 by Eugene H. Peterson. Used by permission of NavPress. All rights reserved. Represented by Tyndale House Publishers.

Scripture quotations are from the ESV® Bible (The Holy Bible, English Standard Version®), © 2001 by Crossway, a publishing ministry of Good News Publishers. ESV Text Edition: 2025. The ESV text may not be quoted in any publication made available to the public by a Creative Commons license. The ESV may not be translated in whole or in part into any other language. Used by permission. All rights reserved.

DEDICATION

This book is dedicated to my husband, Brandon, and my Mama. You saw who I was going to be today, before anyone else (including me) could see it.

CONTENTS

Foreword   7

Introduction   11

Part 1: The First Yes   18

1   The Life You're Living Vs. The Life You're Called To   23

2   The Excuse Factory   47

3   Own Up   65

Part 2 : Lace Up Your Boots   92

4   Faith is Not Safe—And That's the Point   97

5   Obedience > Feelings   117

6   Comfort Kills   137

Part 3 : Embrace the Greatness God Has for You   154

7   You Were Made For More—Act Like It   159

8   The Cost of Your Calling   179

9   When the Dust Settles   199

Conclusion : No More Holding Back   217

Acknowledgements   223

FOREWORD

From the first time we met Jen, we knew she carried something rare. Humility, hunger, and a deep desire to follow Jesus wholeheartedly. We've watched her walk out her "yes" with consistency and courage, and as she leads, you can sense the strength and clarity of her voice to guide others. Now beautifully captured in these pages.

Have you ever felt that quiet, persistent nudge in your heart? That sense that God is inviting you to something more? Not necessarily louder or flashier or easier. Just *more*. More aligned. More surrendered. More alive.

That's the heartbeat of this beautiful and powerful book.

In *Every Yes*, Jen walks us into the deep end of radical obedience. But she doesn't do it with guilt or pressure. She does it with grace, humor, vulnerability, and the kind of authenticity that instantly puts you at ease. Reading these pages feels like having coffee with a wise, funny, Jesus-loving friend who isn't afraid to tell the truth, and who believes, down to her toes, that your life has purpose.

Jen's message is clear: obedience isn't about perfection. It's about presence. It's about courage. It's about trust. Saying yes to God, even when it feels small or scary, is the beginning of everything. And in a world that often celebrates loud ambition or polished success, Jen reminds us that the Kingdom moves through quiet faithfulness. Through obedience when no one's watching. Through the yes that costs us something, and leads to everything.

We love how Jen weaves her story through Scripture, not just as a narrator, but as a fellow traveler. She's walked the long roads of waiting. She's stared disappointment in the face. She knows what it's like to give God a full-bodied yes and then wonder what in the world is happening next. She's lived it, so her words carry the weight of wisdom, not theory. You'll find deep theological truth here, but it's clothed in everyday language that makes it accessible, relatable, and deeply moving.

What makes this book so timely is how it speaks into the hesitation many of us live with. We want to follow God. We want to live on purpose. But we're not sure where to start, or we feel unqualified, or we're just too tired to try again. Jen gently peels back those layers and reveals what's been there all along—a calling. A path. A promise. And a God who hasn't changed His mind about you.

If you've ever wondered whether your story still matters… it does. If you've ever doubted whether you still have time to walk in your purpose… you do. And if you've ever felt like your faith has grown too quiet or too cautious… this book might just be the divine spark you didn't know you were waiting for.

So get ready. Read with an open heart. Let the Holy Spirit breathe fresh wind into your weary places. And maybe, just maybe, by the end of this book, you'll find yourself whispering, *"Yes, God. Whatever it is. I'm in."*

This is more than a book.

It's an invitation.

Let's go.

Holly Wagner - author, pastor

Dr. Donna Pisani - author, pastor

INTRODUCTION

Your next yes is bigger than you think.

What seems small today could shift the course of your life in ways you can't yet see. The question is, will you say yes or ignore it?

The Butterfly Effect is a theory about how tiny actions have ripple effects far beyond what we can see. For example, a butterfly flaps its wings in India, creating a change in air pressure that eventually causes a tornado in Alabama. The theory pertains to the weather, but the same principles apply to our lives. Small changes can cause significant results. While I'm willing to take the weather as it comes, I'd rather be more intentional with the way I spend my life. A single yes to God today could lead to a future you never imagined. But what if you ignore it?

God has already given us everything we need for living a godly life just by knowing him. (2 Peter 1:3) It's all at our fingertips. We have to choose to say yes or walk away.

YOU HAVE A CALLING

Every one of us has a calling on our lives—a purpose to fulfill. Too often, we put so much pressure on finding that *precise* high calling that we miss all of the steps right in front of us. Our purpose seems so big and unknowable because we're looking for this one thing we can put a label on. But truthfully, our purpose has a lot more to do with the sum of the steps we take in obedience day after day than one ultimate destination. It's a continuous pursuit of growth and maturity. I hate to be the bearer of bad news, but growth never stops. Your purpose will continue to bloom and grow over time as you commit to walking with the Lord in the way he's asked us.

> Therefore I, a prisoner for serving the Lord, beg
> you to lead a life worthy of your calling, for you
> have been called by God.
> Ephesians 4:1

Radical obedience WILL unlock your purpose. So, walk in a way that aligns with the call of greatness on your life. Before we get too far into this, I want to confront the thoughts that are already going through some of your minds. Greatness. Calling. Purpose. In the context of following Christ, these words make you think of what? Ministry. But let's realize from the get-go that your calling can be anything. Anything! God wants us to be carriers of his presence in every avenue of life. He has set us up as ambassadors on earth. Official representations of God in a foreign land. It stands to reason that there would be a calling for us to walk into every area of life that occupied by people who need to know Jesus. To be the representative of God in your home, raising your children. In your content creation and wedding planning. In your fitness training and your stock exchanges. If there is an area of life with humans, we, as Christ's ambassadors, are called to go there. So don't allow your mind to convince you that these words don't apply to you. YOU do have a calling, and it's one covered in greatness.

> So we are Christ's ambassadors; God is making his appeal through us. We speak for Christ when we plead, "Come back to God!"
> 2 Corinthians 5:20

THE GUITAR

I grew up in church with a family that made being in church a priority. I was taught to live right, do good, and love others. That was easy for me because I enjoy following the rules. The more rules, the better. And don't break them beside me because I'm not going to be able to handle it very well! However, when life took an unexpected turn and the rules no longer made sense, I embarked on a very different journey.

I had a guitar because, as a teenager, I led worship in the youth group of the church we attended. Other than middle school band, worship was my only experience in creating music, and that felt right. Outside of worship, somehow, music didn't feel right at all. I couldn't explain it then, and I still can't explain it now, but I knew that the music that came from me belonged to God. My life had wandered far from being worshipful, so I didn't do much with music for years. As my story moved on, I eventually pawned my acoustic guitar. Chapter closed, I'll take the cash.

But then things changed. God got hold of my life. It was an interesting season that felt like a huge question mark until one day it became completely clear in an instant. I found Jesus. I didn't rediscover the rules I once knew, but just Jesus.

I broke, and like a switch was flipped, I was changed completely. It didn't take long for me to wish I had that guitar back in my life. I wasn't thinking about a *new* guitar; I wanted *my* guitar. Knowing that I was well past being able to get it back, I went to the pawn shop, hoping with every ounce of hope in my body that it was at least hanging on the wall to buy back.

Well, it wasn't. The guy behind the counter asked me what I was looking for. So, in my most disappointed tone, I started to describe this black jumbo acoustic guitar. He said, "You know, something told me to hang on to that." And came back with my guitar. *MY* guitar! He let me buy it back for the same amount of money he gave me in the beginning.

I sat in my car and just sobbed. I knew this was more than luck. I knew this was God speaking to someone who had just given her biggest "yes!" and radically changed everything about her life to follow him. Someone desperate to discover all of the things she had missed for so long. This was God saying, "I see you."

A butterfly flapped its wings in a pawn shop, and a worship leader realized her calling.

I didn't know it then, but my yes in that moment was one of many small obediences that would continue to unlock my calling. And the same is true for you. Your yes, no matter how small, is a step toward the life God is calling you to. Radical obedience starts with the smallest step. The question is, will you take it?

SHAME CAN'T LIVE HERE

If you have known the call God has on your life and you've walked away from it, let this be a fresh start. There's no place for shame here. Romans 11:29 tells us that "God's gifts and his call can never be withdrawn," and I am proof of that. There was a call on my life when I was young and didn't recognize it because of all of the things we're about to talk about together in this book. God still believes in you. The trick is allowing yourself to believe that is true. Shame says, "The ship has sailed." But God says, "Watch this."

> And I am certain that God, who began the good work within you, will continue his work until it is finally finished on the day when Christ Jesus returns.
> Philippians 1:6

THE PURPOSE OF THIS BOOK

My prayer is that this book will be a tool in the hands of anyone seeking to unlock the full life and purpose that God has called them to. This book will challenge you to recognize the power of your yes. Each chapter will guide you through breaking barriers, overcoming fear, and stepping boldly into God's purpose for your life.

There are so many things that are clearer than we think. There will always be more to discover in the Lord through his Word, but my hope and prayer is that the insights that he has led me to share in this book will spark a passion to know HIM. Not religion, not the rule book, but his character. He has given us all we need to live walking fully in his presence and anointing, and it's written right in the Bible.

We all have different experiences following Jesus. Some are based on church experience, some on family influences, and some on personality. Because of that black and white, rule-follower personality I mentioned, it took me until much later in life to realize that I didn't know Jesus as much as I knew how to do the right things.

But when I discovered Jesus for who he really is, that he was someone to get to know and build relationship with rather than a cruel and lofty judge, everything changed. I fell in love with the Bible. I fell in love with the God of the Bible. I learned how to see who he is through the pages rather than looking for myself in them.

It's my prayer that something I share might spark that realization in you. The passion to know the God of the Bible. The trust that the answers are already there for you in His Word. The same Holy Spirit that inspired the words on those pages is the same Holy Spirit that walks with us every single day. And that same Holy Spirit will guide you through this process.

MY PRAYER FOR YOU

> I pray that your hearts will be flooded with light so
> that you can understand the confident hope he has
> given to those he called—his holy people who are
> his rich and glorious inheritance. I also pray that
> you will understand the incredible greatness of
> God's power for us who believe him.
> Ephesians 1:18-19a

I ask only for honesty as you turn these pages. Not honesty with
me, but with yourself, and with God. We have some inside work to
do to get where we want to go, and you'll never get there by
pretending or overlooking the truth. If you're ready to stop
hesitating and start saying yes to God's leading, let's begin.

part 1

The First Yes

PART 1
The First Yes

There's something holy about a beginning.

It's rarely clean. It's almost never perfect. But it's sacred.

That's what this part of the journey is about—choosing to say yes before we know where the path leads. Before the breakthrough. Before the clarity. Before the outcome we're praying for. It's the first yes. The one that unlocks everything else.

This section of the book is personal for me. It holds some of the most vulnerable pieces of my story. It's where God taught me that obedience isn't about getting what I want. It's about becoming who he's called me to be. I've said yes to God in private, in fear, in disappointment, and eventually, in full surrender. One of the clearest seasons of this came during my journey through IVF. I'll share more in Chapter One, but I'll say this here: each attempt required a new level of obedience. Each no refined my faith. And each yes invited others to witness not just God's power, but his presence in my waiting.

This book is a map for walking with purpose. The purpose God has for YOU. This part of the book lays the foundation for the rest.

We'll start with the kind of yes that changes your posture before it ever changes your outcome. Then we'll explore the way obedience shapes us not just in the big moments, but in the daily ones. Then in Chapter Three, we hold up the mirror. We look at the things that keep us stuck. And we'll acknowledge that responsibility begins with awareness. A map won't get us anywhere if we're pretending to be somewhere we're not.

If you've ever felt like you were made for more, but weren't sure how to step into it, this is where it begins. The first yes doesn't require you to be strong, confident, or fully prepared. It just requires you to be willing. To open your hands and say, "God, I'm in. Even if I don't fully understand."

Before we move forward, let's pause.

This book will ask you to take a personal inventory of where you are right now. Not the you you intend to be, hope to be, or think you *should* be. Where are you actually? Self-awareness can be tricky and challenging at times, but it is imperative. There will always be blind spots. But as much as we can be honest about where we are, the more we are able to grow. There is a path to be found towards what God has for us. Until then, we're just leaving all of the good stuff hidden in a destination on a map that we have no idea how to use.

Before we get started, ask yourself:

• Have I truly said yes to God with all of me?

- Am I aware of what might be holding me back?

- What would change if I actually surrendered?

You don't have to have all the answers yet. You just have to be honest.

The first yes is sacred. It's the door.

And once you walk through it, there's no going back.

But trust me—it's where everything starts to come alive.

01

THE LIFE YOU'RE *LIVING* vs.
THE LIFE YOU'RE *CALLED TO*

What if the life you think is safe is actually the most dangerous place to be?

When the time came that my husband, Brandon, and I were ready to have a child, we were confronted with a story we knew nothing about. The story of trying for years to no avail. The story of pregnancy being just out of reach. Hope, pray, accept all of the advice (wanted and otherwise), grieve the losses when they come, regroup, and try again. Then we were confronted with a question: what now?

THE ILLUSION OF SAFETY

The first time we tried IVF, we told no one.

Not because we were ashamed, but because we were afraid. Afraid of the questions, the expectations, the possibility of being disappointed, and so many people seeing it all unfold. Fearful of having to navigate this journey in front of other people. So we kept it private. I held my breath, hoped in silence, and when the answer came back no, we grieved in silence too.

But then, something stirred in me. I knew God was asking me to let people in. To allow my community to be part of the journey. So when we began our second round, I did something terrifying—I told people. I let them pray. I let them hope. I let them stand beside me in faith, believing for a miracle. And when the answer came back as no for a second time, I was wrecked.

Hadn't I done what God asked? Wasn't obedience supposed to bring a breakthrough? I thought for sure that saying yes to him, letting others into my story, meant I would get the answer I hoped for. But instead, I stood in front of those same people, carrying not a miracle, but another disappointment.

It would have been easy to retreat then. To close myself off and return to a quiet, safe faith. But we had one last try left. One more opportunity to trust, even when nothing made sense. So I doubled down. I painted the room intended to be the nursery, and I prayed there. A lot. I printed out scriptures and put them on the walls. And this time, when we said yes, when we stepped out in faith one more time, we received a yes in return.

We were pregnant.

Here's what I've realized: The most incredible testimony wasn't just in the answered prayer. It was in the waiting. People didn't just get to see God move. They got to see us walk through heartbreak and still choose him. They got to witness faith that wasn't contingent on an outcome. And that's the thing about faith

—it isn't safe. It isn't about controlling the results or ensuring a smooth path. Faith is stepping out when God calls, even when you don't know where it will lead.

When I lived in silence, I suffered in silence. When I became vocal, it didn't guarantee that I would get what I wanted. I still had suffering to walk through. However, being obedient and stepping out of my comfort zone positioned me for something greater than I could see in the moment.

My story may not look like yours, but we all face moments where we must decide whether we will settle in fear or step into the unknown, trusting God's purpose. This isn't just my experience. It's the story of every person who has ever walked in faith from Abraham to Peter and beyond. And just like them, God has anointed each one of us for something specific. He put a calling and a purpose on our lives before we were even a thought.

> I knew you before I formed you in your mother's womb. Before you were born I set you apart and appointed you as my prophet to the nations.
> Jeremiah 1:5

King David echoes that same sentiment in the Psalms:

> You made all the delicate, inner parts of my body and knit me together in my mother's womb. Thank you for making me so wonderfully complex! Your workmanship is marvelous—how well I know it. You watched me as I was being formed in utter

seclusion, as I was woven together in the dark of the womb. You saw me before I was born. Every day of my life was recorded in your book. Every moment was laid out before a single day had passed. How precious are your thoughts about me, O God. They cannot be numbered! I can't even count them; they outnumber the grains of sand! And when I wake up, you are still with me! Psalm 139:13-18

Do you understand how much sand is out there? I've always read this and thought of a beach. *A* beach. But think again about every beach. Now add in all of the deserts. And the golf courses. And the sandboxes. And the goldfish tanks. Everywhere there is sand! That number doesn't even scratch the surface of the thoughts God has for us. It's an absurd amount of sand, which equals an even more ridiculous amount of thoughts! And they're about you! Now, if a human said that, we would think it's a beautiful exaggeration. Well, wasn't that romantic? But it's against the character of God to lie. When he says it, it's true! Our days are carefully planned and written out with purpose and intention. Yes, even *yours.*

Knowing that, why would we settle for less than his best plan? It's one thing if something amazing is being dangled in front of us, but we still have to get through an obstacle course, chase it down, and claim it for it to be ours. But being consecrated and appointed isn't something we've had to search out. It was placed on us before we were ever even conceived. Knowing it's there, it's ours, it's our calling, the way we were created, why would we settle for less?

This is, of course, a big question with different answers for different people. But there is an answer nonetheless. We all have different stories and experiences that develop or produce who we are. Different personalities, upbringings, and journeys we've walked over time that have shaped who we are by nature. But just because we are naturally inclined to be, act, or think a certain way doesn't mean that's what we're destined to be. The worst thing we can do is come to terms with "that's just how I am." What's important to remember is that by nature, we are all sinful people in a fallen world. But that's not our calling! Our nature is not our calling. Our nature is in constant turmoil with who we're called to be because of the sin in our world. Our nature can, and should, be refined. That's what the whole Bible is about. The journey from perfect Eden, to the fall and imperfection, back to Eden. That is the journey we see from cover to cover. God believes the best in his kids even when it makes no sense to do so. He wants to see us back in a perfect relationship with him, like he planned from the beginning.

The hang-up can be that to get back to Eden, to the goodness, it takes being able to fight our nature. To make tough decisions and stand firm. So many are content to settle into what feels like a safe, quiet faith. Choosing to flow with the current, rather than fight to keep a firm footing. Choosing hesitation, silence, or partial obedience, in the thought that it will protect you from pain or disappointment. It's easy to believe that if we hang onto this false sense of control, we can avoid pain in life. But all that leads to is stagnation.

If you've ever seen a pond with standing water, you know it doesn't take long for it to become murky, smelly, and lifeless. Here in the south, stagnant is a word I know to run from! I picture slimy water and mosquitoes breeding. It's about to be bad when you see that going down! Stagnation isn't good for water in your yard in the summer, and it's not good for the water of your soul either. We weren't made to live that life. We are wired for more. The Bible often ties our answered prayers and fulfilled desires to taking delight in the Lord. That's because it's in our wiring to want to be near him. Our soul craves it even when our mind doesn't understand the need and our will doesn't want to make the decision to step out in faith.

Every person we see in scripture who experienced the fullness of God had to step beyond their comfort zone. As we examine examples from the Bible, look for the pattern of running from complacency as they realize that God's plan is better than their own.

ABRAHAM

> The Lord had said to Abram, "Leave your native country, your relatives, and your father's family, and go to the land that I will show you. I will make you into a great nation. I will bless you and make you famous, and you will be a blessing to others. I will bless those who bless you and curse those who treat you with contempt. All the families on earth will be blessed through you." So Abram departed as the Lord had instructed, and Lot went with him. Abram was seventy-five years old when he left Haran.
> Genesis 12:1-4

Abraham was called to leave everything that was familiar. He was called to leave his family and his country and go to this mystery destination that the Lord just teased with, "I'll show ya." With obscurity and a promise, Abraham set out without question or hesitation. One of the most sobering thoughts in Abraham's story comes from a couple of verses before. At the end of Genesis 11, we see Abraham's father, Terah, heading to the land of Canaan. This is the land promised to Abraham and his descendants that we just read about.

> One day Terah took his son Abram, his daughter-in-law Sarai (his son Abram's wife), and his grandson Lot (his son Haran's child) and moved away from Ur of the Chaldeans. *He was headed for the land of Canaan, but they stopped at Haran and settled there.* Terah lived for 205 years and *died while still in Haran.*
> Genesis 11:31-32

Now, there could be a number of reasons Terah wanted to go to Canaan. But I've not come across too many coincidences in the Bible. Did Abraham know his father was called to go to Canaan and didn't follow through? Did he walk into this call from the Lord knowing what settling and complacency looked like? Was this a no-questions-asked "yes" for him because he spent his years in Haran watching passion and life drain out of his father as he gave up his true destination for a place to settle?

Because of Abraham's yes, we inherit a blessing from God. Abraham's yes was much bigger than he realized. God did, indeed, deliver on that promise, and Abraham became the father of many nations. For generations to come, people referred to God as the God of Abraham. But the promise didn't come quickly and easily like you might expect after reacting so faithfully and courageously when God called him. Abraham was 100 years old when he and Sarah finally had their first child! He was 75 when he first received the promise from Genesis 12. That's twenty-five years of hanging on to that promise and being faithful. Even as he watched himself and his wife age with no child to start their family line. Genesis 18 says that Sarah had already gone through menopause! She laughed when they were told it was time for their child because she was "worn out." (Genesis 18:12) That's real life right there. As we delve further into the story in Romans 4, we see that Abraham's promise didn't come easily, but it had a profound and lasting impact due to his unwavering faith.

> Even when there was no reason for hope, Abraham kept hoping—believing that he would become the father of many nations. For God had said to him, "That's how many descendants you will have!" And Abraham's faith did not weaken, even though, at about 100 years of age, he figured his body was as good as dead—and so was Sarah's womb. Abraham never wavered in believing God's promise. In fact, his faith grew stronger, and in this he brought glory to God. He was fully convinced that God is able to do whatever he promises. And because of Abraham's faith, God counted him as righteous.
> Romans 4:18-22

Unwavering faith in a situation where anyone would waver. But Abraham was "fully convinced that God is able to do whatever he promises." That's making a bold decision to believe something seems out of reach just because God said it. That scripture goes on to include us!

> And when God counted him as righteous, it wasn't just for Abraham's benefit. It was recorded for our benefit, too, assuring us that God will also count us as righteous if we believe in him, the one who raised Jesus our Lord from the dead. He was handed over to die because of our sins, and he was raised to life to make us right with God.
> Romans 4:23-25

Because Abraham hung onto the promise of God, moved to an unknown destination, and walked in unwavering faith, the nation that would be God's chosen people was born. And if we believe in Jesus Christ, we are adopted into that family and promise. It was a yes that was weird and hard, but still, today it leaves an impact. Should that have come through his father, Terah? We'll never know. But we know that Abraham had the faith and steadfastness to carry it out.

Thank you, Abraham.

PETER

> Then Peter called to him, "Lord, if it's really you, tell me to come to you, walking on the water."

"Yes, come," Jesus said. So Peter went over the side of the boat and walked on the water toward Jesus. But when he saw the strong wind and the waves, he was terrified and began to sink. "Save me, Lord!" he shouted. Jesus immediately reached out and grabbed him. "You have so little faith," Jesus said. "Why did you doubt me?"
Matthew 14:28-31

To set the stage, it's between 3:00 and 6:00 AM. A crazy storm is raging, Jesus is walking on water towards the boat, and because of a local legend, all the guys in the boat are sure he's a ghost. Jesus says, "Hey, it's me, don't be scared." (Jen paraphrase) Then, Enter Peter. He squints into the mist of the storm and the darkness of the night and doesn't ask a question, but says, "Lord, if it is you, command me to come to you on the water."

We are at the pinnacle of chaos here, and Peter wants to get out of the safe, comfy (maybe not comfy, but at least safe) boat to walk on (not calm) water in the middle of a storm. Something, by the way, they never, until this moment, even knew was a possibility. Jesus tells him to come, and Peter does. He gets out of the boat and walks on the water. Until he doesn't. Until he gets distracted by everything around him. Jesus is right there to pick him up and walk back to the boat with him.

Don't miss the details here. What is powerful to recognize in this story is that when we see Peter sink, we might say, "Shame, shame. You shouldn't have gotten distracted." But you know how Peter reacted? He didn't go to the back of the boat and sulk because he sank, he worshiped with all of the rest of the disciples because they could see that "Truly you are the Son of God." (verse

THE LIFE YOU'RE LIVING VS. THE LIFE YOU'RE CALLED TO

33) Peter could have played it safe, but he would have missed the opportunity to experience something truly miraculous. Would Jesus have told Peter to come onto the water if he was going to drown? No. He was his friend. He was his teacher. Jesus knew that the power was there for Peter, but it was up to him.

When we read scriptures like...

"For I know the plans I have for you," says the Lord. "They are plans for good and not for disaster, to give you a future and a hope."
Jeremiah 29:11

And

And we know that God causes everything to work together for the good of those who love God and are called according to his purpose for them.
Romans 8:28

...we have to consider the full context of these verses. Yes! His plans are absolutely good (Perfect, in fact!) for us! He will work all things out for what he has planned for you. IF you get out of the boat. IF you come when he calls you. I haven't read any accounts in the Bible where God rewarded someone for their outstanding job of attending synagogue every week and simply existing. He calls us to more, and when you step into the "more" that he's called you to, it affects so much more than you can see in the moment. Because Peter decided to do something radical, something seemingly impossible, everyone present was led to worship! Everyone present experienced something miraculous that night as Jesus walked back to the boat with Peter. The storm calmed, and the presence and power of God hit them with amazement, which resulted in worship. The only proper response!

Way to go, crazy Peter.

THE RICH MAN

In contrast to our other two stories, here we find someone who chooses safety over surrender.

> As Jesus was starting out on his way to Jerusalem, a man came running up to him, knelt down, and asked, "Good Teacher, what must I do to inherit eternal life?" "Why do you call me good?" Jesus asked. "Only God is truly good. But to answer your question, you know the commandments: 'You must not murder. You must not commit adultery. You must not steal. You must not testify falsely. You must not cheat anyone. Honor your father and mother.'" "Teacher," the man replied, "I've obeyed all these commandments since I was young." Looking at the man, Jesus felt genuine love for him. "There is still one thing you haven't done," he told him. "Go and sell all your possessions and give the money to the poor, and you will have treasure in heaven. Then come, follow me." At this the man's face fell, and he went away sad, for he had many possessions.
> Mark 10:17-22

This is a heartbreaking story because we can see that the man was so excited! So eager. He has followed the teachings of the Torah his whole life. But Jesus called out his distraction. His roadblock. The one thing that was more important to him than God's calling. Wealth is what is in the way for this man. We know that's not always the specific case for each person. God doesn't have an aversion to wealth in itself. I have seen people who have been blessed with great wealth and a generous heart to go with it. Realizing they've been blessed to be a blessing.

We also know that God doesn't require us to sell everything we have. In fact, in Luke 19, we see the story of Jesus talking with a man named Zacchaeus. He was a "notorious sinner," and Jesus called his name and asked to spend time with him. Zacchaeus gets so excited that he exclaims he is going to give half of his wealth to the poor, and Jesus is pleased. (Luke 19:1-9) This story isn't about money, but about heart. In the same way, the command for the rich man to sell all of his possessions wasn't about the money at all. It was about removing the idol in his life that was keeping him from a full commit.

There are many things that we can hold in our lives or hearts where this guy held his wealth. What is it for you that would make you walk away from Jesus sad because you couldn't give it up? What would be just too hard to let go? It can be a difficult reality to confront, but greatness never comes without cost. But that cost comes with a promise. And for those committed to following Jesus, it changes the perspective. We may not know what it will look like on the other side of obedience, but we do know it will be worth it.

> Jesus replied, "And I assure you that everyone who has given up house or wife or brothers or parents or children, for the sake of the Kingdom of God, will be repaid many times over in this life, and will have eternal life in the world to come."
>
> Luke 18:29-30

True faith has never been about eliminating risk. It has always been about trusting God enough to step into the unknown.

WHY DO WE SETTLE FOR LESS THAN GOD'S PLAN?

As we look at these stories of faith and discover warnings about holding too tightly to things that can build a wall between ourselves and God's best plan, where do we find ourselves on this spectrum of faith? If we know we are called to more, why do so many of us settle? How do we avoid the response of the rich man and live like a Peter or an Abraham? Let's look at some of the most common reasons people settle. As you read, take note of where you find your hang-ups that might be getting in the way of radical obedience.

Fear of Failure

This one won't be a surprise to anyone. Common to all people in all areas of life, no one wants to be, or be seen as, a failure. No one wants to be a disappointment or look inadequate. That's a fair concern. I don't either.

Fear of Success
Yep, that's right. Some settle for less because of a fear of success. When they realize that success requires greater responsibilities, higher expectations, and more effort, many may be reluctant to pay the price of success. Some people subconsciously avoid success because they fear they won't be able to maintain it or that it will change their relationships.

Low Self-Worth
We'll reference this one multiple times in this book because it's a passion point of mine. So many feel they aren't good enough for more. That they don't deserve more. Or in the "picked last" mentality, it's just not in the cards for them. Someone who believes they don't deserve better will settle for what they think they can get rather than what they're truly capable of achieving.

Comfort and Complacency
Chapter 6 is dedicated to this one. Comfort is one of your biggest enemies in the quest for being all you can be. Comfort convinces us that everything is just fine the way it is. Complacency tells us that "just fine" is good enough and there's no reason to strive for change. We are called to be content, but not complacent. And those are very different. But it's easier to stay where things are predictable and manageable rather than face the discomfort of change. People often choose familiarity over potential.

Lack of Vision
For one reason or another, some cannot see where they should be heading. A quote from Helen Keller says, "The only thing worse than being blind is having sight but no vision." Whether you make

a conscious decision to move or not move, you've decided. You put yourself on a path to your next destination every day of your life. Without a clear sense of purpose or a compelling vision for the future, people drift through life without striving for more.

Negative Influences or Discouragement

This plays a significant role in self-worth, but often, people, including those who *seem* close to you or *should* be your cheerleaders, speak negative words over your dreams, hopes, or goals. Family, friends, or culture may send the message that pursuing more is unrealistic or selfish. This can be hard to accept as reality when it's someone you love who is the source of the negativity, but the following quote is true on every level and should be pasted to your mirror if this is where you find yourself:

> "An athlete won't judge you for working out. A millionaire won't judge you for starting a business. A musician won't judge you for trying to sing a song. It's always the people going nowhere who have something to say."
> - Unknown

Past Disappointments

Failed relationships, dreams that haven't materialized, church hurt, spiritual betrayal. There are many things from the past that can linger, affecting our mindset and hindering our ability to move forward. Sometimes, with what feels like an unanswered prayer, you can be afraid to step out again. You may have failed at the business you were called to start before, so this time you're worried. You may have tried to share your faith and been rejected.

The plans you've made didn't work out like you hoped, so you're nervous to go down that road again. When people experience repeated failures or setbacks, they may begin to believe that trying again isn't worth the effort. They internalize past pain as proof that they'll never succeed.

Lack of Spiritual Depth

Many settle for less in life because they settle for less in their walk with God. Unless you're walking in a growing relationship with Jesus, it's understandable that you might not be looking for more yet. Everything starts with step one: falling in love with him, not just in theory, but in a deep, personal way. As that relationship grows, things begin to awaken in your spirit. If the voice of the Holy Spirit feels unfamiliar right now, I pray this book becomes a spark—an invitation to lean in and listen. The presence of the Holy Spirit in your life isn't meant to feel distant or reserved for someone else. It's meant to feel like home. And once he feels like home, he becomes the force that pulls you toward everything God created you to become.

Disobedience

You know who you are if this is you! Some know deep down what God is calling them to, but they resist because it requires sacrifice. They settle for a lesser path that feels safe, rather than walking in obedience. They know God has called them to do something, and they're just not doing it. They either ignore it altogether or keep praying for an answer, knowing full well that he isn't going to tell them to do something new when they haven't done what he's already asked. If this is you, don't beat yourself up. You're holding a book in your hand right now that is meant to help you over this hump. We're here doing the work. Read on, and let's grow through it.

Time

Let's call this for what it is. This is busyness. This is distraction. This involves making choices to do what you want with your time, rather than what you're called to do with it. We are all given the same 24 hours every single day, and within that time, some people move mountains, and some conquer a Netflix series. It's all about choices. A theme that will keep coming up, as it turns out.

Sports aren't bad. All video games in themselves aren't bad. Social media isn't inherently bad. Entertainment isn't inherently bad. But when we have stretched schedules and we finish out the hours of our week with all of these things that are simply a disposable choice we're making with our time, we can't then look at God with our hands thrown up in the air saying we don't have time for what he's asking.

Comparison

This is a trap that we have all fallen into at some point in our lives. This one can stop you in your tracks fast if you let it take hold. There will always be someone who can do something better than you. There will always be someone with an "easier" story. Someone more capable, better at speaking, more popular, this list could go on forever in whatever category we're looking at.

Don't let comparison take root or you will never do anything of worth.

Right about the time I had this game on lock, I started writing my first book. (Welcome to my journey of growth!) Ask me if there are a million books out there that are better than this one. Of course! But letting the enemy use that to shut me down would have been denying what the Lord asked me to do.

In anything you are called to do, there will be a million more people doing that thing. But not one of them is you. Not one of them can combine that thing with your personality, your calling, your experiences, and your spirit. Don't let comparison take root, or you will never do anything of worth.

As we look at this list of things that cause so many to settle for less than what God intends for us, where do you recognize yourself? You're likely to resonate with more than one category. Where have you been playing it safe? What fear has kept you from fully trusting God? Whether you actively choose to move forward or stay where you are, *you are making a choice*. Every day, you either step closer to your calling or further from it. Let's choose to live like a river, not stagnant mosquito water. Recognizing where we are and where we need to heal and grow sets us up for an on-purpose journey, so be honest. This is good work.

THE POWER OF SAYING YES

Every person who has experienced deep transformation in the Lord has had to step beyond what is comfortable. In every area of life, we have to be willing to put down the good to take hold of the great. The same is true with our faith. Hesitation is often the greatest barrier to experiencing full life in Jesus. What if Abraham had hesitated? What if Peter had stayed in the boat? What if they had chosen comfort over calling? Their choices didn't just impact their lives; they impacted generations.

So what if your yes is bigger than you think?

WHAT'S HOLDING YOU BACK?

Where have you been playing it safe? What fear has kept you from fully trusting God?

Maybe it's time to stop asking for permission. Perhaps it's time to step forward even when you don't feel ready.

When the Lord had a transformative moment with people in the Bible, he often changed their names. A name is very telling of the person and who they will be. How they will live, and the mark they will leave on the world. When we found out that our miracle baby was going to be a boy, we wanted to choose a name that would set him on an intentional path. A persona that we felt the Lord had for him. We chose Asher Jaxon. Asher means happy and blessed, and Jaxon means that the Lord has been good and shown us favor. And it has all been true. He can tell you what his name means because we speak it over him, and have since he was tiny.

What name has been spoken over you? For a long time, my name was "worthless." It was "unlovable." It was "unwanted." It was "disposable." But I'll never forget the moment when God said, "No, that's not your name." And the more I learned of God as I read his Word, the more my mind understood what he says of me, and how different it was from what I had heard.

I don't want you to overlook this thought just because maybe no one has said anything hateful to you before. Having a name you need to shed doesn't necessarily mean you've had a bad life experience. It doesn't even have to mean someone else has spoken it. Many times it does, but we carry a lot of self-inflicted labels. "I'm not enough." "I'm broken." "I'm not qualified." "I'm not like them." "I'm not a leader." "I'm too late." "I'm just…" You're never "just" anything when you're walking with Christ! Not *just* a mom, not *just* a teacher, not *just* an accountant, not *just* anything! To be able to walk in the power Jesus has for you, you have to let Jesus change your name.

You may call yourself unworthy, alone, basic, unloved, depressed, orphaned, too much, not enough…shall I go on? You may call yourself a lot of things. But, God has called you set apart (Jeremiah 1:5). He has called you his child (1 John 3:1). He says that you are his handiwork (Ephesians 2:10), redeemed (Isaiah 43:1), liberated (Galatians 5:1), created in his image (Genesis 1:27), and forgiven (1 John 1:9). He has called you chosen. CHOSEN! (1 Peter 2:9) Am I the only one who needs to know that one super loud?

There are scriptures upon scriptures in the Bible of amazing things God has spoken over you. The best part of taking on these descriptions over what you may have believed of yourself so far is that these don't come from our strength at all. It's all because of Jesus. None of us is good enough on our own, or redeemed on our own. So take the pressure off and take on your true calling. Take some time, before we move on, to recognize the label that is hanging over you. Reject the lie. Then replace it with the truth. If I didn't hand you a scripture to combat the lie here, look it up! There will be one to hang on to! There are so many more words of purpose and life spoken over you than what any human has spoken over you. But they only hold enough weight to outweigh the negative if you realize who's talking to you.

For the Lord is a great God,
a great King above all gods.
He holds in his hands the depths of the earth
and the mightiest mountains.
The sea belongs to him, for he made it.
His hands formed the dry land, too.
Come, let us worship and bow down.
Let us kneel before the Lord our maker,
for he is our God.
We are the people he watches over,
the flock under his care.
If only you would listen to his voice today!
Psalm 95:3-7

This is who has put a calling and a purpose on your life. *This* is who has great things written in your story. How audacious of us to say we're not good enough when the Lord of Heaven said that before we were even a thought on earth, he set us apart and appointed us? There's a calling that you may be ignoring, second-guessing, or haven't realized yet, and wherever you land on the spectrum, our goal is to dig into it and get your steps headed on a path that will bring it to life. The question isn't if you are called—it's whether you will answer.

A FINAL CHALLENGE

You were not meant to live small. You were not meant to stay hidden. Faith is never safe, but it is always worth it. So what will you do with that truth? Will you stay where you are, or will you step into the unknown, trusting that the One who called you is already there waiting? The choice is yours.

02
THE EXCUSE FACTORY

The person who really wants to do something finds a way;
the other person finds an excuse.
-Author Unknown

WHAT IF THERE WERE NO EXCUSES?

What would your life look like if there were no excuses? If you truly responded to every situation in life honestly. Spoke truth, acted accordingly, did the work, admitted the inadequacy, whatever the situation calls for. We would realize that we make more excuses than we think. We would also likely recognize that people are a lot more forgiving of the truth than of an excuse. What if, starting today, you stopped saying 'I can't' or 'I don't have time,' and instead took full ownership of your choices? What would change?

Excuses have been in play since the utter beginning.

The man replied, "It was the woman you gave me who gave me the fruit, and I ate it." Then the Lord God asked the woman, "What have you done? "The serpent deceived me," she replied. "That's why I ate it."
Genesis 3:12-13

Man blames woman. Woman blames serpent. But God saw the whole thing. We can become so accustomed to making excuses that we sometimes even fool ourselves into believing the narrative we present is true. I remember a season of life where my answer was always that I was too busy. I didn't have time for anything else. Then one day, I just realized that I wasn't too busy at all! I said I was busy when, in fact, I hadn't prioritized my time well and was stressed out. Yes, I accomplished a lot. Yes, I had long lists of things to do. But it was all well within reasonable hours and effort if I was being a good steward of my time. After realizing this and correcting my language, it still took years to retrain people not to be nervous about asking me for something because "I know you're so busy."

So what does it take to shut down the excuse factory? The place where we convince ourselves we're doing our best, even when we know there's room for more. It takes a whole lot of honesty, seasoned with a little vulnerability.

WHERE ARE YOU?

A GPS is an excellent tool for direction. But if you're trying to convince the GPS that you're somewhere you're not, you're never going to get to your desired destination. The same goes for walking in your purpose. Progressing to the ultimate destination God intends for you requires us to ask some honest questions and respond with honest answers. You need to determine your true starting point. Not where you *wish* you were starting from, but your actual current status. We're trying to identify the starting point of who you are. Not the person you want to be or "should" be. But who are you right now? Have you been honest with yourself every day about why you have or haven't accomplished a goal? Why you have or haven't been spending time with the Lord?

Remember, through this process, we're wanting to be brutally honest with ourselves, but we're not letting shame and condemnation enter the picture. Recognizing the truth isn't just about coming face to face with our shortcomings, but about coming face to face with the next right step. Shame has no place in the growth process, so go ahead and recognize that it's a trap you're not going to fall into.

The beautiful thing about life IS the process of growth. Thank the Lord for growth! I used to be the QUEEN of excuses! Not to say I never slip one in presently, but I had myself fooled pretty good once upon a time. And truthfully, it all came from a good place, which made it harder to realize and fix. I am a creative person, and I have always loved creating great atmospheres that convey a theme or evoke a feeling. That translates into home design, my wardrobe, and hosting parties. At our church, it translates into platform set design and photo booths, and creative building projects. I would work tirelessly to make sure everything at the church was up to my standards. Straight lines. No smudges. Always changing.

After one too many irritable moods that came along with working way too late in the night, pushing a deadline, and getting bailed out by people who had no intention of dedicating their bedtime to nailing boards to a wall, it was time for a conversation. Jen, you have to loosen the reins. Put it down.

The movie Frozen wasn't out back then, but I know I would have had a theme song if it had been! "Let it go! Let it goooooo." I held on so tightly to so many things because "no one would pay attention to the details like me." "I don't have anyone to help." (Lies) But that led to making excuses in other areas. "I'm too tired." "I'm tapped out." "I don't have time." "I don't have the resources."

A friend I worked closely with at the time told me that if someone else can do a job 80% as well as I can, I need to let it go. Let. It. Go? For less than perfection? Are you kidding? (Insert list of excuses why that was a bad idea here.) But I finally realized that the people who were close to me cared as much about me and the church as I did, and they wouldn't destroy me (on purpose). So I listened. Then began the most painful process of following the advice I was given. As I painfully watched things being done at around 80% as well as I would have liked, I cried a bit. I fumed some. Then I realized that the world kept turning. That people still loved the finished product. That people were still moved by it, excited by it, and more people got to be involved. That, in turn, meant that more people were walking in their purpose as well. Funny thing, when I let go of one overwhelming thing that I was white knuckling for dear life, my capacity was freed up for higher-level thinking. All of the excuses began to fall away as I listened to people around me. That's when my purpose had room to grow.

Here are some questions that can prompt self-discovery in this area. Ask yourself:

- If your time and energy were like a bank account, where are you making the biggest "withdrawals"? Are they investments in what truly matters?

- What habits do you justify even though you know they aren't helping you grow?

- What's one thing you say you don't have time for, but if you truly wanted it, you could make time?

- If you stopped making excuses today, what's the first step you would take toward real change?

EXCUSES AND SELF-DECEPTION

> Because of the privilege and authority God has given me, I give each of you this warning: Don't think you are better than you really are. Be honest in your evaluation of yourselves, measuring yourselves by the faith God has given us.
> Romans 12:3

As you walk through this process of asking questions and taking stock of where you are right now, if you've been honest with yourself, it's likely you realize you have made excuses in different areas. The most common excuse I have heard over the years, and as I have admitted, one I have also been guilty of using myself, is time. I don't have the time. But in reality, we make time for what we want to make time for. Every single one of us has the same number of minutes in a day, and some invest them wisely, while others don't. And even though we all make our own decisions for how to use our time, we tend to look at others who are achieving something we would like in our own lives and say the famous phrase, "That must be nice." Have you ever said that? "Must be nice to have all of that free time." "Must be nice to have so many opportunities just come to you." "Must be nice never to have to deal with anything difficult." "Must be nice to be popular, rich, skinny, successful…" You get the picture.

I made up my mind years ago that I wouldn't use the phrase "that must be nice" anymore. It was a light bulb moment when that line was used on me. I realized that just as that person was not taking into account the work it took to achieve the "nice" thing they were seeing, I didn't know what that work looked like for anyone else either. It's so easy to look at the outside of someone else's story and feel like something you envy or are aspiring to must have come easily to them because that's all you see—that moment. However, behind amazing things are usually countless hours of good decision-making, sacrifices of time and money, determination, and dedication to reaching a goal that sometimes separates them even from their friends. Comparison fuels excuses. But the truth is, people who achieve what we admire weren't given a shortcut—they made different choices.

When you see someone who looks like they must be God's favorite, what you aren't seeing is the time spent in prayer. The love for studying what his Word says. Making decisions that are counter-cultural so they can remain standing firm in the way Jesus asks us to live. God doesn't have favorites. But just like human relationships we have, you are more or less close to the person (or God in this case) depending on the time spent investing in the relationship. The Bible tells us in 1 Timothy 4:16 to "keep a close watch on yourself." Not on other people. What you see in other people is between them and God. You never know the full story of someone else's journey. How are *you* doing? Without excuses. Have you ever seen someone succeed in something you wanted, and instead of making excuses or dismissing the hard work or determination that may have been involved, you asked them how they did it? What if we replaced envy with curiosity?

> Pay careful attention to your own work, for then you will get the satisfaction of a job well done, and you won't need to compare yourself to anyone else. For we are each responsible for our own conduct.
> Galatians 6:4-5

On any given day... Did you have time to scroll on your phone? Did you have time to press the snooze button? Did you have time to go to Target? Did you have time to watch TV? Then you have disposable time that you can restructure to achieve what you want to achieve — *if* you want to. These aren't bad things to do in themselves! Not at all. I love some good downtime. We all have to recharge. We all need to Sabbath. But when the sneaky downtime that isn't profiting our overall goals begins taking over, it has crossed a line from a healthy refreshing moment to a trap from the enemy to keep you from doing what will help you grow and accomplish the thing you're meant to do.

So, what does your time look like? How well are you stewarding your moments? Like Galatians tells us, we are all

What if we replaced envy with curiosity?

responsible for our own conduct. How can you answer for yours? Are your days full of things that are just taking up space? Or are they filled with things that are edifying? Are there things that are bringing your family together or sending them off in different directions? Are there things that are your *best* yes, or just a yes because you *can* say yes? There's nothing that will keep you from the great like what is good. And there's nothing that will keep you from seeing the difference between the two like staying busy. Time is just one way we deceive ourselves into the excuse factory, but it's the easiest and most common trap by far. Whatever excuse-habit you may be in, it's time to shut it down. More often than you think, the people around you can see through the excuses. And we know they don't fool God.

> Don't excuse yourself by saying, "Look, we didn't know." For God understands all hearts, and he sees you. He who guards your soul knows you knew. He will repay all people as their actions deserve.
> Proverbs 24:12

He already knows the heart of every decision you make, and will not bless you out of bad decisions. How betrayed do you feel right now when you realize that it's you? It's you that you're fooling. It's you who has lessened your impact. It's you who has prevented you from growing in your gifts and calling. Your very worst enemy is often just...you. But if you're reading this right now, you have the wherewithal to make this the end of that story. It's time to get to the bottom of it and change the narrative.

RECOGNIZING THE VOICES WE FOLLOW

Whose voice do you know the most? Whose voice will you follow? Let's get honest again. Not whose voice you *wish* you put first. Not who you *wish* you were that familiar with. But let's look at our lives honestly as we sit today and ask those questions. If you're having trouble answering, look at the fruit. What is your life producing? Can you see a pattern of walking with Jesus and obeying his call? Or do you find yourself playing small to fit in with the people around you? Do people come to you for encouragement or because they have a juicy story to tell?

> You can identify them by their fruit, that is, by the way they act. Can you pick grapes from thornbushes, or figs from thistles? A good tree produces good fruit, and a bad tree produces bad fruit. A good tree can't produce bad fruit, and a bad tree can't produce good fruit.
> Matthew 7:6-18

You can't slap an excuse on why a tree is producing apples instead of lemons. Well, friend, it's just an apple tree. The fruit of your life and your relationships will tell the story of which voice is the loudest to you. It takes some honest personal inventory to say, "Wow, culture has a really loud voice in my life." "I find myself more worried about people and appearances than I do about what the Lord thinks." If you're someone who wants to walk in your purpose and make an impact, this isn't a fun thing to discover about where you are. The beautiful thing is how quickly you can make a shift if you make up your mind to change. It's called repentance.

If you have this book in your hand, I'll assume that you know Jesus. Maybe not the way you want to know Jesus, but we're (hopefully) headed in that direction. Therefore, you're probably familiar with the term "repentance." It's to turn in a new direction. To commit to course correction. And when you do that, it's a moment of recalibrating that GPS we talked about before. Recognizing where you are so you can make the correct turn ahead and start making steps down the right path. The only way to drown out the world's voice is to amplify God's.

When we recognize that we may be following the wrong voices in our lives, we must learn to lean into the right one. We'll look further into how to do this in chapter 3, but know that in the middle of all of the voices around you, when you know the voice of Jesus closely, you'll be able to follow even his whisper.

EVEN THE FAMOUS ONES MADE EXCUSES

When we look through the Bible, we can see many examples of people making excuses instead of just giving a loud and hearty "Yes!" While we can read these stories and think, "Man, didn't you realize that you were talking directly with God?!" I am so grateful that these stories are included for us to read. If all we saw were perfect leaders and earthshakers, it would all feel a bit daunting. But we get to see how God used people who made excuses to go on to do amazing things. However, I do always think back on the stories and wonder what might have been different if they had not hesitated.

I don't know how many times I've been driving and veer from the GPS directions, to keep hearing "recalibrating... recalibrating... make a U-turn when possible... recalibrating." I know that at that moment, I'm adding time to my journey, one missed turn at a time. Feeling myself go the longest way possible to a destination, I can't help but think about Moses. His "should have been short, but took 40 years" journey is a story for another day, but he was a famous excuse maker in the Bible who went on to lead in an amazing, history-shaking way.

Moses is one we know pretty well. His story from birth was a miracle, and covered with the hand of God. Saved from a death sentence as an infant, rescued from abandonment in a river by Pharaoh's daughter, returned to his biological mother to be raised as a child, then grew up in the home of Pharaoh. His story is nothing short of amazing! Wrapped in purpose. But when it's time for Moses to walk into the big moment, leading the Israelites out of slavery, he drew back in the most human and familiar way.

He had all of the excuses–"But God, they won't listen to me!" "Who am I anyway??" "They won't believe that you have spoken to me." So, God tries to give Moses some confidence by showing him miraculous signs that he can perform to convince the people that he is telling the truth and was indeed sent by God. I mean, really cool, miraculous things. God has him throw down his staff, and it turns into a snake. Then he was told to pick it up again, and it turned back into a staff. God had Moses put his hand in his coat and pull it out, and it was covered with leprosy. He had him put it back again, and it was healed. Not your everyday happenings! But even after these crazy things happen, Moses says, Yeaaaaaaah, but for real. "I am not eloquent, either in the past or since you have spoken to your servant, but I am slow of speech and of tongue." (Exodus 4:10) So God gets super ticked at Moses and tells him to bring his brother to be the public speaker, God would give his words to Moses, and Moses can tell Aaron to speak them out loud. Whew. What a mess. What would have been different if Moses had just realized that God wouldn't call someone that he didn't equip? That he might actually know what he's doing?

That is one of the hardest things for most people to grab hold of and accept as true in their lives. If God has called you (and he has), he has equipped you. Just like God says to Moses through his excuses, "Who makes a person's mouth? Who decides whether people speak or do not speak, hear or do not hear, see or do not see? Is it not I, the Lord? Now go! I will be with you as you speak, and I will instruct you in what to say." (Exodus 4:11-12) The power, the strength, the confidence, doesn't come from ourselves. We have to trust that God has called us and allow him to do the work in us and through us. He just wants us to take him at his word and say yes.

> If you trust the God you follow, you can trust his call on your life.

God will make this happen, for he who calls you is faithful.
1 Thessalonians 5:24

Where does your "but God" statement come in? What do you know you feel called to do, but you're allowing limiting thoughts to keep holding you back? Explaining away your hesitation with one excuse or another. We say we trust God in so many ways. We trust he will provide for our needs. We trust him for our salvation. We trust that he provides peace in the midst of chaos. We trust that he will show up for others. However, we can often lack the same trust that he will show up for us when it comes to our calling. The lack of faith in that area may come from insecurities or other excuses about why he wouldn't do something amazing for you. But the truth is, the God who called you is faithful. You have no right to feel low when he has called you higher. If you trust the God you follow, you can trust his call on your life.

Moses had every reason to believe he wasn't the right guy for the job. But God never asks for qualifications, only obedience. When Moses came with excuses, how did God respond? He asked Moses, "What's that in your hand?" (Exodus 4:2). It was a staff. The staff he had been walking with for who knows how long. It was already with him. It was already part of him. Moses, let's start with what you have. Offer back to me what you already have. That hasn't changed today. What's the thing you feel unqualified for

Don't forget that words like "calling" and "purpose" aren't exclusive to positions in the church. Being "called" may not be a vocational ministry at all. It likely isn't! It may be in the medical field or working with technology. It may be teaching or developing a successful business that will fund ministry and missions. It can be common to think that to do what God has called you to do means walking away from the thing you love and walking towards ministry. But what it really means is walking closer to the Lord, and what you love either becomes full of purpose, or he shows you new avenues of passions that are inside of you that you haven't even tapped into yet. Ministry can be found in every moment, in every career path, and in every hobby, if you're doing it with God's leading.

that He's already called you to do? When we offer back what we have, however small it feels, God will make it count. What might have been different if Moses had said "yes" immediately? What would change if you trusted God's equipping instead of your own limitations?

PRESSING ON – NO MORE EXCUSES

> No, dear brothers and sisters, I have not achieved it, but I focus on this one thing: Forgetting the past and looking forward to what lies ahead, I press on to reach the end of the race and receive the heavenly prize for which God, through Christ Jesus, is calling us.
> Philippians 3:13-14

Living life without excuses takes intentionality. We won't always like the truth about how we've acted, used our time, invested our creativity, or taken the long way around to what God has for us. However, it's worth being honest with ourselves so that we can take the right steps forward. It's time to press on. Sometimes pressing on from a moment. And sometimes from the things from our past that have set us back. Remember that your past is just that. Your past. And it can stay there *if* we allow the work of Jesus to take root in our lives. My past has been good, bad, ugly, wonderful, and devastating. But if I cling to the good or am held prisoner by the ugly, I am missing what lies ahead. We have all messed up at some point. Many of us have been set back by the words or actions of others. But nothing that has happened so far is the end.

My past, like many, includes words being spoken over me that were devastating. Words that took years to heal. Words that in my weak moments still haunt me. But the work of Jesus says, "That's not too much for me. Do you think we can't walk this out together? Come on, let's go. What matters now is that you don't ever go back there and that you remember what *I* have said about you. It's time to press on, and we'll do it together."

When I fell in love with Jesus, I prayed that I would remember enough of my past so that I never forget what He has brought me through, but forget enough to be able to forgive myself and act like the new creation that I am. He has answered that prayer in the most beautiful way. My heart grieves deeply when I am around people who follow Jesus and *should be* rejoicing in new life, but are reveling in the darkness of what used to be. Telling the stories of their past with fondness, and remembering the good 'ol days. I don't mean to be a prude about it, but I feel like that part of our lives shouldn't be where we find our funniest stories. That is a person I want to put away, heal from, and this new me (and you) is where the best part of it all will be. These are the days that will produce the best stories to tell. The ones that will live on and on and be a pleasure to tell. The stories that will encourage and inspire. The stories that will long outlive our time on earth.

Forget the past. That means if someone told you you're not good enough. Forget it. If someone told you you'll never measure up. Forget it. If someone has spoken failure, worthlessness, or abandonment over you, press on. If someone has made you feel stupid or less than or unlovable, press on. There is so much greater ahead! IF we forget the past and look forward to what is ahead. Let go of past labels and press on. What is the thing from your past that you find yourself clinging to? What has crept so deeply into your being that you don't even realize it has taken residence as a part of you, even though it has no business being there? Like I said, honesty isn't always fun, but it's necessary to realize where we really are. Are you willing to stop letting excuses define you? Are you ready to step into the purpose God has for you without hesitation?

You have a choice. Continue making excuses, or step fully into what God has in store for you. No more hesitating. No more waiting for the perfect moment. Just say YES. What's your move?

03
OWN UP

When the Lord saw that he turned aside to see, God called to him out of the bush, "Moses, Moses!" And he said, "Here I am."
Exodus 3:4 ESV

As a shepherd, I'm sure Moses had his usual stomping grounds. I picture him having walked by that bush many times before. But on this day, something stopped him. The passage doesn't say God called him over. It says he waited until Moses turned aside. That detail hits me every time. It makes me wonder: how many times had God tried to get his attention before? And how many times do I keep walking when God is trying to get mine?

Sometimes, I imagine God going, "Jen. This bush is on fire. Will you stop?"

The entire premise we're working towards in this book is to understand and take hold of what God is calling us to do, and walk fully and powerfully on that path. But we can't take responsibility for our calling if we can't even see it right in front of us. Just as we discussed the GPS before, we have to recognize our current location before we can proceed where we're called. That awareness, that moment of turning aside, is where it begins.

Here's the thing: turning aside doesn't always look like a dramatic moment. It doesn't always look like fire. Sometimes it looks like a gut feeling you can't shake. Sometimes it looks like hesitation that doesn't make sense. And sometimes it looks like trusting the Holy Spirit when no one else understands why.

Many people live in frustration, as though God isn't at work. He's likely moving all around you, but you're not tuned in to see it or hear from him. There is a new joy and life that come when you are tuned into the way he is speaking to you in your regular, everyday life. I was talking with someone recently who began taking note of the little things in their day that directly confirmed a prayer they prayed that morning. Everything, down to a worship song quietly playing during a doctor appointment, was an answer to the prayer. A detail that would be so easy to miss if you're consumed with worry or striving to find the answer. Have we postured ourselves to be ready to see, hear, and receive direction from the Lord?

We can all be prone to having spiritual blind spots. But those blind spots can be dangerous because they keep you from seeing how evident God's presence already is in your life. They come in different forms and keep us from seeing how God is already moving. Some come from distraction. We're too busy to notice. Others stem from denial. We resist what we know he's asking. And sometimes, we rely on others instead of seeking him for ourselves. Each one keeps us from stepping fully into responsibility.

What might you be ignoring that God has already placed right in front of you? How can you work to get rid of the blind spots that might be keeping you from seeing it?

Moses had to *turn aside* before he could receive what God was calling him to. If he hadn't noticed, he might have walked right past his purpose. Are you aware of what God is doing, or are you walking past it? Just as Moses had to turn aside, we must *choose* to be spiritually aware. Sometimes the process of discovering what that looks like for you unfolds in an interesting way.

There was a moment early in the life of Cultivate Church when I experienced this in real time. I am the worship pastor, so the need for great musicians is a weight I feel to my core. We had a guy come who wanted to play piano with us, so we started him in our developmental program. He could play well, but there was something that I wasn't settled on. Our pastors, people on the team, everyone felt great about him. Everyone except me. I kept making excuses for why he needed to stay in developmental, putting him off until he finally got fed up and quit developmental. Let's just say that in the early life of a church plant, the pastors weren't excited about my decision. Almost immediately after that, we hear that he was leaving the church because he got a job as the worship leader of a church down the road. Sorry guys.

Within a couple of months, we received word that he had been unfaithful to his wife and they were getting a divorce. Jaw on the floor. That's never easy to hear about someone. I still didn't attach it to my uneasy feeling, or protection over our worship team, but a great friend on our team called it out. Jen knew. She listened to the Lord and protected our team from the emotional fallout of the wrong person in the wrong role over our church. Could my eyes have gotten any bigger as he spoke? Nope. However, since it was called out, I became aware of what had been there all along. That was a turning aside moment. I just didn't know I was turning. The unease I couldn't name was the Holy Spirit. That hesitation wasn't me dragging my feet—it was God pulling me close. Speaking. Guiding. Protecting.

Like Moses, I could've kept walking. I could've ignored the unease, pushed him through the process, and hoped for the best. But God was already speaking. I just needed to recognize it. As I've learned to lean into what the Lord is doing in my life, I've learned that spiritual awareness requires a few things from us.

Stillness

When we're busy striving, searching, and trying to fill the time on our own until we "hear from God," we completely miss how God is already at work. Slow down. Pray the prayer, then trust that God will open your eyes to see.

Openness

Be willing to receive whatever it is that God is revealing to you. What God has called you to isn't always going to be what you imagined or thought it was going to be. Great things come with a cost. Growth comes with pruning. There might be a part of what he is revealing to you that sounds scary, but be open enough to realize that God will accomplish what he sets out to accomplish, and there is no weakness of ours that will get in the way, and no difficult moment that he won't walk us through.

Honesty

Some of us already know. We know we're gifted as intercessors, but we're staying isolated. Some of us are gifted as leaders, but are doing less, so less will be required of us. Some of us are gifted as teachers or mentors, worship leaders or small group leaders, but are drawing back because of the accountability that comes with it. Honestly admit when you've been avoiding responsibility for what the Lord has called you to.

Once we become aware, we can no longer pretend we don't know. Awareness demands a response. Once Moses turned aside, God called his name. When we step into awareness, we step into responsibility. Once we take ownership of our awareness, the next step is learning to recognize how God speaks. If we aren't tuned into his voice, we can't follow his direction.

RECOGNIZING GOD'S VOICE

We hit on how to recognize what voice is getting the platform in our lives in chapter 2. Now let's lean into how to recognize God's voice above all of the other voices in our lives. This can be difficult because there are so many voices, and they all have a lot to say! Some are very obviously the wrong voice. Some are there just to slip in enough doubt to cause you to freeze. (This is the sneaky one.) Some voices will be that of a friend who is trying to be helpful, but ends up adding to the noise. The trick is learning which voice is our own, which voice is a friend, which is the Enemy, and which is the Lord. We can find comfort in Scripture. We *can* know his voice above the rest.

But the one who enters through the gate is the shepherd of the sheep. The gatekeeper opens the gate for him, and the sheep recognize his voice and come to him. He calls his own sheep by name and leads them out. After he has gathered his own flock, he walks ahead of them, and they follow him because they know his voice. They won't follow a stranger; they will run from him because they don't know his voice.
John 10:2-5

When we learn to recognize the voice of Jesus clearly, all other voices stick out and feel out of place. Why? Because we've spent enough time with the right voice. The voice of the Shepherd. The guidance of the Holy Spirit won't be a shouting presence. He won't force his way in. But when you know it, you can stand firm knowing that you are walking in truth. How well do you recognize God's voice in the noise of life? Could you pick it out as easily as a child recognizes their mother's voice?

When a baby zebra is born, something really special happens to make sure that he knows his mother better than any other zebra. Zebras all have different stripes, much like our fingerprints. When a baby zebra is born, mom takes the baby just a little bit away from the herd so the baby can learn to identify her. This is a big deal! The whole point of a zebra's stripes is to distract predators from picking out one zebra to attack. The stripes confuse them, and they more or less get dizzy and give up! But the baby is able to pick out Mom in that ocean of stripes. Why? Because before the baby knows any other stripes, it knows mom's. Like a baby zebra, we have to spend time alone with our Father to know his voice before we involve any others.

One of my favorite comforting and confidence-building scriptures is found in Isaiah:

> Your own ears will hear him. Right behind you a
> voice will say, "This is the way you should go,"
> whether to the right or to the left.
> Isaiah 30:21

He's there guiding you when you make the decision to let his voice be the loudest. But the caveat to this guidance comes earlier in the chapter:

> So the Lord must wait for you to come to him
> so he can show you his love and compassion.
> For the Lord is a faithful God.
> Blessed are those who wait for his help.
> Isaiah 30:18

It's up to us. God is always ready. He's waiting not with frustration, but with expectation. He's eager to open up a world of purpose and calling to those who will slow down, turn aside, and choose him.

But here's the thing: we won't hear his voice by accident. There will always be other voices: louder ones, flashier ones, familiar ones. And if we're not careful, those voices will drown out the still, steady call of the Shepherd.

We learn to hear his voice by spending time with him. Consistently. Intentionally. Not just when we're desperate or when life falls apart, but as a daily rhythm. It's like any relationship. The more time you invest, the closer you become.

We don't get to default our way into discernment. We have to choose it.

We don't get to blame distraction forever. We have to fight it.

We don't get to hide behind culture's expectations. We have to rise above them.

We each have a decision to make: How will I invest my time, attention, and affections? Because at the end of the day, it comes down to that. Not excuses, just choices. And every choice has consequences. What voices influence you the most? God or culture?

So many times I hear people ask, "Why won't God speak to me?" But maybe he already has. Maybe the answer you're looking for has passed by a dozen times. Maybe it's lying right in front of you. God does speak. He speaks through his Word, his Spirit, his people, and his creation. But he's not always going to set the bush on fire.

There's a misconception that we have to beg, strive, or perform just right to hear from him. But the truth? It brings him joy to speak to his children. You don't have to force it. You just have to posture yourself to hear it. The path is already laid out. He's already speaking. The question is, are you listening?

God does speak. But he's not always going to set the bush on fire.

"When you come looking for

me, you'll find me. Yes, when you get serious
about finding me and want it more than anything
else, I'll make sure you won't be disappointed."
God's Decree.
Jeremiah 29:13-14 MSG

When you get serious about finding God and want him more than
anything else, you won't be disappointed. The important thing here
is not just wanting the blessing or the answer to a prayer. It's when
you want HIM more than anything else that you will not be
disappointed.

HOW DO WE RECOGNIZE GOD'S VOICE IN OUR EVERYDAY LIVES?

God Speaks Through Scripture

The first, easiest, most clear, in-your-pocket, comprehensive way
is the Bible. The Word of God. Once upon a time, you had to read
every single word by candlelight to find what you were looking
for. Now it's on your phone. It's everywhere. There are endless
tools to help you read, study, and apply it in ways that make sense
for your life right now. But because it's everywhere, it's easy to
take for granted. Out of all the writing in all the world over all
time, these are the words inspired by the Holy Spirit. Given to help
us know the character of God, understand how he moves, and
recognize the gifts he's placed in our lives.

Paul said, "Let the word of Christ dwell in you richly…"
(Colossians 3:16a). That word "dwell" means to be at home in us.
It's not something we visit occasionally, but it lives in us. We draw

from it because it's become part of us. That kind of relationship with the Bible comes from reading it consistently. Even when you're just reading out of obedience, even when it feels dry, it's still shaping the way you see and know God.

That's easy to do when life is going well. When you're in a groove with your reading plan or digging into a study that fits your season. But what about when you're spiraling with worry? When you're desperate for answers? Are you in the Word then?

Sometimes the answer is yes. But often, it's no. Reading Scripture is often the first thing to fall away when life gets hard. But it's exactly when you need it most. If I'm counseling someone on one of my teams and they aren't reading the Bible, it's a full stop for me. Not because I'm frustrated, but because there's nothing I can say that will be more powerful than what God has already said.

> For the word of God is alive and powerful. It is
> sharper than the sharpest two-edged sword, cutting
> between soul and spirit, between joint and marrow.
> *It exposes our innermost thoughts and desires.*
> Hebrews 4:12

The Word of God will show you things you didn't know about yourself. It will speak to your purpose, expose what's blocking your growth, and breathe life into places that feel dry. But Scripture isn't the only way God speaks.

God Speaks Through Prayer

Prayer is how we stay connected to the heart of God. It's not just about bringing a list of requests. (Although he cares deeply about those.) It's also about listening. About sitting with God, asking him to speak, and actually making space for a response. Many people don't pray because they think they don't know how. But it's not complicated. Prayer is simply talking to God, just as you would to a trusted friend. You don't have to use the right words or say things a certain way. You can pray in your car, on a walk, with a journal, or just sitting in silence.

Want a starting point? Try something like this:

- "God, I want to hear you. Speak to me in a way I can understand."

- "Help me recognize your voice over the noise."

- "If I've been missing something you've already said, bring it back to my mind."

And then pause. Don't rush off. Sit in that moment. God isn't in a hurry, and you don't have to be either.

> God isn't in a hurry, and you don't have to be either.

Make Time to Be Alone with God

Another key way to hear his voice is to make space for him to speak. That means getting quiet and getting alone. It's not always easy in a busy world, but even Jesus did it. He often withdrew to quiet places to pray (Luke 5:16). Solitude isn't about isolation. It's about focus. It's about tuning out distractions so you can tune in to the voice that matters most.

Sometimes God speaks through a verse, sometimes a whisper in your heart, and sometimes through a deep sense of peace or discomfort. Sometimes it's clarity, and other times it's just the quiet reassurance that he's with you. But you won't know if you don't make room for it.

The Prompting of the Holy Spirit

Another way God speaks is through the Holy Spirit's prompting. This can be easy to overlook because it requires stillness and awareness. You have to be paying attention. It may feel like a check in your spirit when something's off. It may feel like peace when nothing else makes sense. It may be a sudden insight, or even someone else's words standing out to you like they were meant just for you.

> When the Spirit of truth comes, he will guide you into all truth. He will not speak on his own but will tell you what he has heard. He will tell you about the future.
> John 16:13

> Then he added, "Pay close attention to what you hear. The closer you listen, the more understanding you will be given—and you will receive even more."
> Mark 4:24

The Spirit will never contradict the Word. The more familiar you are with Scripture, the more clearly you'll be able to recognize when he is speaking.

This isn't a comprehensive list of all the ways God speaks. Not even close. But it's a starting point. You can open your Bible. You can have an honest conversation with God. You can get quiet and pay attention. You can do all of that today.

When you're walking closely with Jesus, the Holy Spirit has room to guide you. You'll be able to sense when something is right or when it's not. With that career move, that opportunity, that next step, you'll feel peace or tension. You'll see confirmations in your day that help guide you. That's not just your gut. That's the Holy Spirit.

So let me ask you this: Are you listening, or are you waiting for something dramatic like a burning bush?

EXCUSES VS. OWNERSHIP

Everything that God has called us to is hanging in the balance: whether we make excuses for why not, or take ownership and move forward. I'm hoping this book is the tipping point that helps you make a move towards your purpose.

Think back to Moses. He had a strong grip on all of the reasons he was not cut out for what God had set before him. But the whole narrative changed when he decided to just go for it. We get to see a close relationship where Moses walked with God every step of the way, and God provided for every need along the way.

We get a birds-eye view of Moses, making it easier to see how all the steps play out. But we just get the up-close view of our own lives. Waking up with the same insecurities to fight today that we had yesterday. Wondering where our next yes will lead us. Even when we are walking in what God has called us to, we are sometimes, as a mentor of mine puts it, oblivious to the obvious. To us, it is clear that God is moving in miraculous, history-marking, world-changing ways in the life of Moses. Why not in our lives?

Take another look at Moses's story from a zoomed-in point of view. As a person, Moses had to wake up every day and lead a stubborn group of people through the desert day after day. The miraculous is clear in the zoomed-out view, but probably wasn't as clear in the day-to-day in the desert. Once he dropped excuses and started walking in purpose, he still had to take ownership of that journey every day, even when it was the most frustrating. It's a funny story to read because when things go wrong, he gets aggravated with God for sticking him with these crazy people. (They were close like that.) But he had to work through the daily grind just like the rest of us.

Moses wasn't the only one who wrestled with excuses. Jesus told a story about servants entrusted with responsibility, and their response determined their future. This parable provides a clear picture: we either take ownership of what God has given us or we sit back and waste it.

> Again, the Kingdom of Heaven can be illustrated by the story of a man going on a long trip. He called together his servants and entrusted his money to them while he was gone. He gave five bags of silver to one, two bags of silver to another, and one bag of silver to the last—dividing it in proportion to their abilities. He then left on his trip.

The servant who received the five bags of silver began to invest the money and earned five more. The servant with two bags of silver also went to work and earned two more. But the servant who received the one bag of silver dug a hole in the ground and hid the master's money.

After a long time their master returned from his trip and called them to give an account of how they had used his money. The servant to whom he had entrusted the five bags of silver came forward with five more and said, 'Master, you gave me five bags of silver to invest, and I have earned five more.'

The master was full of praise. 'Well done, my good and faithful servant. You have been faithful in handling this small amount, so now I will give you many more responsibilities. Let's celebrate together!'

The servant who had received the two bags of silver came forward and said, 'Master, you gave me two bags of silver to invest, and I have earned two more.'

The master said, 'Well done, my good and faithful servant. You have been faithful in handling this small amount, so now I will give you many more responsibilities. Let's celebrate together!'

Then the servant with the one bag of silver came and said, 'Master, I knew you were a harsh man, harvesting crops you didn't plant and gathering crops you didn't cultivate. I was afraid I would lose your money, so I hid it in the earth. Look, here is your money back.'

But the master replied, 'You wicked and lazy servant! If you knew I harvested crops I didn't plant and gathered crops I didn't cultivate, why didn't you deposit my money in the bank? At least I could have gotten some interest on it.'

Then he ordered, 'Take the money from this servant, and give it to the one with the ten bags of silver. To those who use well what they are given, even more will be given, and they will have an abundance. But from those who do nothing, even what little they have will be taken away. Now throw this useless servant into outer darkness, where there will be weeping and gnashing of teeth.'

Matthew 25:14-30

The master entrusted each one with a responsibility in accordance with their abilities. "Entrusting" means to commit to someone with confidence. The master wasn't flippantly taking a chance on the guy he gave the least to. I'm sure he had plenty of other servants he could have given money to if he was just being random. He knew this guy could handle that responsibility properly.

What's noteworthy here is that when the third servant came back and hadn't done anything worthwhile with his entrustment, the master didn't say, "Aww man. That stinks. Well, at least you didn't lose anything." No, an entrustment is a formal bestowing of responsibility. And this guy blew it. It can seem harsh that he was punished so severely in this situation, but the master knew he had the capability to do the work and just didn't.

When God calls you, he's not dropping a random request on a person who may or may not be able to hit the mark. When he calls you to something, it's because he knows you have the capability. Dropping the excuses and taking full ownership and responsibility of our calling and purpose amounts to much more than just doing a task for the Kingdom of God. Our master, God, has formally bestowed responsibility on us by entrusting us with a calling. We all have some role to play in helping humanity find him and build relationship with him. And we see in scripture that he takes it very seriously. We even see that there will be different degrees of welcome into heaven based on how we handle our calling here on earth.

> But on the judgment day, fire will reveal what kind of work each builder has done. The fire will show if a person's work has any value. If the work survives, that builder will receive a reward. But if the work is burned up, the builder will suffer great loss. The builder will be saved, but like someone barely escaping through a wall of flames.
> 1 Corinthians 3:13-15

This letter (to the Corinthians) is to the brothers and sisters. To people in the Church who follow Jesus. And he says that on judgment day, our work will be tested. Our works don't save us, or lack of works take away our salvation. But they will be tested, and those who have been good stewards of what they were entrusted with on Earth will receive a greater reward than those who were poor stewards of their time and calling. Can you imagine the feeling of getting to heaven and suffering great loss? That doesn't even seem possible. But it is.

This is why we need to take radical ownership of what God has entrusted to us. Our faith, our actions, and our mindset. What has God entrusted you with? What are you doing with what God has already given you?

SCRIPTURE AS THE FIRST STOP—NOT THE LAST RESORT

I mentioned earlier that if I'm counseling someone and they are not reading the Bible, it's a full stop. Yes, part of that is that I have a very no-nonsense approach to life (and I'm not a counselor), but most of it is that I know that God has spoken plainly to us in his Word and there's nothing I can say to trump the voice of God. Call out truths? Yes. Help clarify based on the way God has revealed himself to me through his Word over the years? Yes. However, I can't be the source for someone any more than your pastor or mentor can be for you. We are responsible for our own growth. Of course, the beautiful thing about this is that we're still not meant to do it alone! We're built for community. We learn and grow so much in conversations with other believers. But you have to be plugged into the source, and so do they. We're called to be iron sharpening iron (Proverbs 27:17), not the blind leading the blind.

> We're called to be iron sharpening iron not the blind leading the blind.

There is a lot that can be learned and understood through the parables of Jesus. The parable of the sower is one that I have thought through in so many ways from so many angles. When you role-play from every different element of the story, you learn so many things. But for now, we're thinking through the soil. Let's read the story together first:

> He told many stories in the form of parables, such as this one:
>
> Listen! A farmer went out to plant some seeds. As he scattered them across his field, some seeds fell on a footpath, and the birds came and ate them. Other seeds fell on shallow soil with underlying rock. The seeds sprouted quickly because the soil was shallow. But the plants soon wilted under the hot sun, and since they didn't have deep roots, they died. Other seeds fell among thorns that grew up and choked out the tender plants. Still other seeds fell on fertile soil, and they produced a crop that was thirty, sixty, and even a hundred times as much as had been planted! Anyone with ears to hear should listen and understand.
>
> Matthew 13:3-9
>
> The seed that fell on the footpath represents those who hear the message about the Kingdom and don't understand it. Then the evil one comes and snatches away the seed that was planted in their

hearts. The seed on the rocky soil represents those who hear the message and immediately receive it with joy. But since they don't have deep roots, they don't last long. They fall away as soon as they have problems or are persecuted for believing God's word. The seed that fell among the thorns represents those who hear God's word, but all too quickly the message is crowded out by the worries of this life and the lure of wealth, so no fruit is produced. The seed that fell on good soil represents those who truly hear and understand God's word and produce a harvest of thirty, sixty, or even a hundred times as much as had been planted!

Matthew 13:19-23

It's no mystery that in the hierarchy of soil in this story, we want to be the good soil. But how do we take ownership of our faith in such a way that we're always receptive to the Word of God? Not only that, but being a good steward of the calling we've been entrusted with so that we produce a crop that is thirty, sixty, and even a hundred times as much as we plant? I think it has a lot to do with fertilizing our soil. With refining our soil. Working the land like any farmer would when they want the soil to be ready to receive seed and grow deep roots.

When it comes to the soil of our hearts, that looks like building a deep, rich relationship with Jesus. It looks like *remaining* in him. Not having passing encounters with him.

All Scripture is breathed out by God and profitable
for teaching, for reproof, for correction, and for
training in righteousness, that the man of God may
be complete, equipped for every good work.
2 Timothy 3:16-17 ESV

The Scriptures are breathed out by God, which means the words
contained in the Bible are infused with the very essence of our
Creator. How do we get to know him and his character? By falling
in love with the Word of God. We've already talked about how
easily accessible the Bible is these days. But instead of regarding it
as common, it should be seen as such a gift. Not a feature added to
our phones. When Jesus walked the earth, people had to memorize
the Scripture because they couldn't afford to have their own copy.
They would study in the temple and remember and recite and pass
down the words. It would dwell in their hearts and minds. It
transformed everything they did and thought because they *knew* it.

And you must commit yourselves wholeheartedly
to these commands that I am giving you today.
Repeat them again and again to your children.
Talk about them when you are at home and when
you are on the road, when you are going to bed
and when you are getting up. Tie them to your
hands and wear them on your forehead as
reminders. Write them on the doorposts of your
house and on your gates.
Deuteronomy 6:6-9

THIS is how we are to hold the Word of God.

TAKING RESPONSIBILITY FOR OUR SPIRITUAL GROWTH

Just like no one can download the Word of God into your spirit and mind for you, no one can do the work of spiritual growth for you either. There are no scriptures that point us to a pastor to grow us spiritually. Pastors are called to shepherd, to watch over, to equip, to lead, guide, serve, and oversee. But none call them responsible for an individual's growth. However, there is a list of scriptures that instruct us to do that ourselves.

> Dear friends, you always followed my instructions when I was with you. And now that I am away, it is even more important. Work hard to show the results of your salvation, obeying God with deep reverence and fear. For God is working in you, giving you the desire and the power to do what pleases him.
> Philippians 2:12-13

God gives us everything we need to live a godly life, but he doesn't force it on us. We're invited into a partnership: one where our effort and his Spirit work together in beautiful tension. Paul tells us to "work hard," not because salvation is earned, but because it's expressed through how we live. We prepare the soil. We pull the weeds. We water the roots. And while we do, the Holy Spirit begins to produce something deep within us. Something we could never manufacture on our own. "For *God* is working in you,

giving you the desire and the power to do what pleases Him."
(Philippians 2:13) We work out what God has already worked in.

The fruit of the Spirit—love, joy, peace, patience,
kindness, goodness, faithfulness, gentleness, and self-control—is
not the result of striving, but of surrender. It grows in the heart that
is yielded, cultivated, and obedient. The Spirit doesn't produce
fruit in hardened soil. He grows it in lives laid open. So while you
are working (obeying, trusting, showing up), the Spirit is working
too. Pruning what doesn't belong. Strengthening what does. And
producing fruit that lasts.

> Since we are living by the Spirit, let us follow the
> Spirit's leading in every part of our lives.
> Galatians 5:25

Are you hungry for spiritual growth, or do
you expect someone else to spoon-feed it to
you?

We work out what God has already worked in.

When we are babies, we need
someone to feed us. Our parents or
caretakers make sure that we are fed enough times a day to help us
grow and stay nourished well. But there comes a time in life when
that same parent starts teaching us to feed ourselves, and they
begin feeding us less and less. Then comes the point where we are
solely responsible for feeding ourselves. If we're malnourished as
adults, that's not our parents' fault. I would never think to call my
mom and tell her I don't want to be her child anymore because I
wasn't fed today, and she should have made sure that happened.
But that's what happens in church. If someone has been in a season

of isolation or has pulled back from serving others, it's not long before the call comes. "I'm not getting fed here." Not that community and serving guarantee things will be perfect, but pulling away from those things is a tell-tale sign of a bigger issue. Jesus never said, "Sit and wait for someone else to feed you." He said, "abide in me" (John 15:4) and "work hard" (Philippians 2:12). These tell-tale signs mean it's time for question asking. The book of Hebrews addresses this very issue, and the writer certainly doesn't take responsibility for the lack of growth among the people.

> You have been believers so long now that you ought to be teaching others. Instead, you need someone to teach you again the basic things about God's word. You are like babies who need milk and cannot eat solid food. For someone who lives on milk is still an infant and doesn't know how to do what is right. Solid food is for those who are mature, who through training have the skill to recognize the difference between right and wrong.
> Hebrews 5:12-14

Maturity means picking up the fork. We are to abide in the Father. That's intentional (John 15:4). We are to fan into flame the spiritual gifts we've received. That's work (2 Timothy 1:6). To have your gift of discernment trained by constant practice. That's also work (Hebrews 5:13). So, what are you doing to take responsibility for your spiritual growth? Are you spending time in God's word daily? Are you spending time in prayer? Are you applying what you've learned? Feed yourself.

I learn a lot about growth through keeping plants. There is no plant I've ever kept that flourishes and grows on its own with no help. (I've also seen exactly what happens when no care is given. R.I.P.) It requires water, fertilizer, and the right amount of sunlight. Some of them even require a sweet conversation here and there, along with a little petting. Whether they're a little work or a lot of work, none of them (not even a snake plant) grows with no care at all. Your spiritual growth takes work, just like growing a plant does. We need prayer, scripture, and community. If you feel spiritually stagnant, ask yourself: Am I tending to my own growth, or am I just expecting it to happen on its own?

FROM CONSUMERS TO CONTRIBUTORS

True discipleship isn't just about being fed but about feeding others. Just like that scripture in Hebrews begins, "You have been believers so long now that you ought to be teaching others. Instead, you need someone to teach you again the basic things about God's word." (Hebrews 5:12) When you watch someone grow in their faith there is, what I think, the coolest transition that happens when someone has grown to a point where they turn the tables and start to give back.

I work with the recovery program in our church. It's such a cool ministry to be a part of because you get to witness so many stories of life change. Witnessing the journey of someone who finds Jesus, grows in their faith, begins healing from their past, and ultimately reaches a point where they're ready to give back is my favorite part of serving with that ministry. And to be honest, it happens a lot more easily when people have encountered the life-changing power of Jesus and not allowed themselves to forget it. When you are fully aware of what Jesus has done for you, it's a no-brainer next step to turn around and serve so that others can experience the same thing. Don't become so complacent in your walk with Jesus that you forget how much grace and mercy you have received. (And still receive regularly!) Maturity isn't just about taking in. It's about giving back. You know you're growing when your first thought shifts from 'What am I getting?' to 'How can I serve?'

Maturity means picking up the fork.

When we think about our spiritual growth, do we have a 'me' mindset or an 'others' mindset? Growth comes when we shift from expecting to be served to serving others. What is one step you can take this week to own your spiritual growth?

If you've been waiting for someone to feed you, it's time to pick up the fork. God has already set the table. Will you come and eat?

part 2

Lace Up
Your Boots

PART 2
Lace Up Your Boots

It's time to get to work!

You've taken the time to look inward. You've sat with truth, wrestled with resistance, and named the things that have held you back. That's no small thing. However, self-awareness was never meant to be the destination. It's the launch pad.

Here's the truth: knowing the direction is not the same as walking the road. You can sit with the map forever and still go nowhere. There comes a moment when the information you've gathered has to translate into motion. This is that moment.

Part Two is about movement. It's about obedience that shows up in your calendar, conversations, priorities, and posture. It's the part where your theology becomes your testimony, where faith takes form. Not just in what you believe, but in how you live.

God isn't asking you to understand everything. He's asking you to trust him enough to take the next step. The steps won't always feel easy or logical. You may still have questions. But radical obedience was never about having complete clarity. It's about having complete surrender.

You weren't created to simply believe differently. You were made to live differently. And that happens one choice, one step, one act of obedience at a time. Walking out a life that makes an impact requires a determined spirit. One bent on making each decision with the end in mind. Fortunately, we're not meant to do that alone. We're making each decision with God right by our side.

> Don't be afraid, for I am with you.
> Don't be discouraged, for I am your God.
> I will strengthen you and help you.
> I will hold you up with my victorious right hand.
> Isaiah 41:10

With our source of strength in mind, let's charge ahead. If you're tired of circling the same mountain, if you're ready to stop admiring the idea of purpose and actually step into it, then let's go. The compass has done its job. Now, let your feet follow.

There's work to do. And it's holy work.

04
FAITH IS NOT SAFE—
AND THAT'S THE POINT

Faith is to believe what we do not see, and the reward of this faith is to see what we believe.
–Augustine

Think back to the story of Peter walking on water. Would we have thought he had great faith if he stayed in the boat and just felt in his heart that he could probably walk on water with Jesus? No.

What would we say of Moses's faith if he just said no and kept moving his flocks? Would we even know his name? Not likely.

What if faith isn't just belief, but movement? What if unlocking our purpose isn't "owed to us" but comes at a cost?

FAITH DEFINED

Faith is one of the core elements of following Jesus. Of believing the Bible. Of trusting God. The dictionary version of faith is "strong belief in God or in the doctrines of a religion, *based on spiritual apprehension rather than proof.*" The biblical definition of faith is often quoted from Hebrews 11:1: "Faith shows the reality of what we hope for; it is *the evidence of things we cannot see.*"

Faith can be a challenging topic in my neck of the woods (America). There is a big difference between Western thinking and Middle Eastern thinking. When we look at the context in which the Bible was written, it's worth noting the thought processes that were present in the writers. Those would be the same thought processes of the people learning at that time it was penned. In Western thinking, we want to understand something before we believe it. In Middle Eastern thinking, it's the opposite: I believe, and then I will seek to understand.

That is why Jesus taught in parables rather than opening Scripture in a classroom setting, dissecting the meanings as we would in Western culture. The people believed in God and his instruction, so he taught through stories (parables) to illustrate the deeper meaning of what they believed, so they could understand the heart of it all.

Dare I say the Middle Eastern way of thinking takes a lot more faith, while Western thinking is more likely to just put faith aside? It's definitely too hard to make it make sense before deciding to follow Jesus full tilt. You have to jump in with faith, or you probably won't jump at all.

FAITH DEMONSTRATED

Great acts of faith often shake history. At the very least, they change the course of a person's life. The greatest acts of faith we see in the Bible involved risk. In one hand, a person holds the hope of an answered prayer, healing, or new life. In the other hand, the realization that they could walk away at the least, disappointed, and at the worst, dead. (Middle Eastern culture didn't play around back then.) However, in the cases we read about in the Bible, the risk seemed worth it to them, and in the end, it paid off immensely.

Faith is belief in something we cannot see, therefore cannot prove, so naturally, it's risky. But your next step of faith could at the least change your life, and at the most, the lives of many others. Faith is active trust in God. Will you be bold enough to take the risk and say yes to what God is speaking to you?

We have the benefit of being able to look at some amazing examples of faith which provide encouragement for our own faith journey. Sometimes we can look at these huge stories of earth-shaking faith and wonder how their stories fit into our own. But there are also stories we see that didn't move mountains, but did create a ripple effect that echoed into the future just the same.

Faith often requires pruning. Cutting away fear, hesitation, and comfort to step fully into God's plan. Let's look at some biblical examples where faith required action before understanding.

A DOG, A LESSON, AND A PEEK INTO THE FUTURE

In Matthew 15, we find the story of a woman who stepped into a conversation she had no business being in, and asking for help from someone who, culturally, she had no business asking.

> "Then Jesus left Galilee and went north to the region of Tyre and Sidon. A Gentile woman who lived there came to him, pleading, "Have mercy on me, O Lord, Son of David! For my daughter is possessed by a demon that torments her severely."
>
> But Jesus gave her no reply, not even a word. Then his disciples urged him to send her away. "Tell her to go away," they said. "She is bothering us with all her begging."
>
> Then Jesus said to the woman, "I was sent only to help God's lost sheep—the people of Israel."
>
> But she came and worshiped him, pleading again, "Lord, help me!"
>
> Jesus responded, "It isn't right to take food from the children and throw it to the dogs."
>
> She replied, "That's true, Lord, but even dogs are allowed to eat the scraps that fall beneath their masters' table."
>
> "Dear woman," Jesus said to her, "your faith is great. Your request is granted." And her daughter was instantly healed."
> Matthew 15:21-28

At first glance, this interaction is pretty rough. Man, I didn't know Jesus was so cold! But when we look at this story in context with the rest of Matthew 15, we see that Jesus had been trying to drop hints that the Gentiles were going to be included in his ministry. But people just didn't get it. Not the disciples. Not the other rabbis. No one was catching on. So far, Jesus had just been ministering to Jews, and it would be the opposite of every Jewish tradition they had ever known to think Gentiles would be included in God's blessings.

Just before this story, in verse 16, Jesus shows his exhaustion in trying to get them to see the big picture when he says to Peter, "Are you still without understanding?" I picture so many question marks and exclamation points here! (We'll never know because the original languages that the Bible was written in didn't have ANY punctuation! But I can only imagine.)

Then we see this woman come along. A Gentile–someone who has not been a focus of Jesus's ministry yet. So was he testing her motives in his reaction, or just making a point to the disciples? Maybe both. Her answer showed that she knew the heart of God better than they expected, even though she had no reason to expect a favorable reply. The way this conversation unfolds results in this woman's bold faith teaching a lesson that would shake the foundation of everything the disciples had known so far.

As she trimmed away the cultural limitations that would have held her back from Jesus, the disciples began the process of pruning off limitations on God's promise. They started cutting away cultural norms to see the world as God sees it. All because of this woman's faith. The way was paved for Matthew 28:19 when Jesus commanded us to go into all the nations to make disciples.

She got an answer to her hopeful request. Her daughter was healed instantly. But her act of faith also opened the eyes of the disciples to look past their prejudices and current cultural limitations. What if she had ignored the urge just to ask? She knew her lesser status because she commented on the scraps that fell from the table. What if she had let that get in her head? What if she had not said "yes" to this act of faith, but stayed in her culturally acceptable place as a woman and a Gentile? Her daughter would not be free, and she wouldn't have experienced the grace of Jesus when his tone changed to "dear woman."

> What if your next step of faith will reach farther than you could imagine?

What if your next step of faith will reach farther than you could imagine?

Just like the Gentile woman's faith broke cultural expectations, Abraham's faith challenged the very promise God had given him. Both stories remind us that faith often demands action before it is fully understood.

A PROMISE, A KNIFE, AND A WILLING SACRIFICE

We've talked about Abraham before. He was called to leave everything he knew to set out for a brand new life. That in itself was a bold act of faith! Traveling to an unknown destination, trusting that God was going to lead the way. That's pretty big. But the plot thickens. After being promised to be the father of many nations, Abraham and his wife, Sarah, were unable to have a child. After much drama and turmoil, they finally have a son. Isaac. Then

102

God puts Abraham to the test and tells him to go sacrifice his son as a burnt offering.

Come again??

We know from reading the Bible that that is completely against God's character. Red flag number one. But Abraham didn't have the benefit of reading the Bible to learn about God's character. He was a part of making history at the moment.

Without a moment of hesitation, Genesis 22:3 says that "Abraham rose early in the morning" to get to his assignment. Of course, there comes a point where Isaac is adding up the details of the journey and asks, "Where is the lamb for the burnt offering?" (Dad always forgets something. Eye roll.) But Abraham doesn't even put the worry on his son. His second huge act of faith in this story, he responds that "God will provide for himself the lamb for a burnt offering, my son." (verse 8)

They arrive at their destination and... no lamb. No replacement for Isaac. Sweat. Panic. Ok, God. Abraham stacks the wood, ties Isaac, and lifts the knife. Fully surrendered to God's command. The son he was finally blessed with is about to be gone in the most awful, gut-wrenching way possible.

But just in the nick of time...

At that moment the angel of the Lord called to him from heaven, "Abraham! Abraham!"

"Yes," Abraham replied. "Here I am!"

"Don't lay a hand on the boy!" the angel said. "Do not hurt him in any way, for now I know that you truly fear God. You have not withheld from me even your son, your only son."

Then Abraham looked up and saw a ram
caught by its horns in a thicket. So he took the ram
and sacrificed it as a burnt offering in place of his
son.

Abraham named the place Yahweh-Yireh
(which means "the Lord will provide"). To this
day, people still use that name as a proverb: "On
the mountain of the Lord it will be provided."
Genesis 22:11-14

Cutting it a little close there!! Can you imagine the faith it took to
walk in obedience to that very last moment? But Abraham went
with complete faith that God would show up and be faithful just as
he always had. Before the full picture was in focus. Before he
knew the details. Abraham had to prune the parts of himself that
would want to hold on tight to his promised son. He had to die to
his way of thinking to follow the God that had blessed him with
Isaac in the first place.

Well before God intervened, when he and Isaac headed
towards the mountain for the sacrifice, Abraham told the guys that
were with them that *they* would be right back after they had
worshiped on the mountain. He knew the God he served was good,
but that didn't take away the risk. That didn't take away the fear.
But he said yes, knowing what was at stake.

And because of his yes…

The angel of the Lord called again to Abraham
from heaven. "This is what the Lord says: Because
you have obeyed me and have not withheld even
your son, your only son, I swear by my own name

that I will certainly bless you. I will multiply your descendants beyond number, like the stars in the sky and the sand on the seashore. Your descendants will conquer the cities of their enemies. *And through your descendants all the nations of the earth will be blessed—all because you have obeyed me."*
Genesis 22:15-18

Talk about an amazing impact! That reaches all the way to us today! We are blessed because Abraham took a huge risk and had faith in God.

What if your next step of faith will reach farther than you could imagine?

FAITH APPLIED

Think through the examples we've looked at. Picture yourself in their shoes. Could you have stepped out of the boat? Would you have been able to spark a desperate conversation with Jesus? Would you have been able to trust God to save your child? We were never called to sit still in our salvation. To have faith and just wait for Jesus to come back. No, faith demands action. By following Christ, we join in his mission, and he calls us to action.

"*Prove by the way you live* that you have repented of your sins and turned to God. Don't just say to each other, 'We're safe, for we are descendants of Abraham.' That means nothing, for I tell you, God

can create children of Abraham from these very stones."
Luke 3:8

We were never called to sit still in our salvation.

God doesn't *need* us to accomplish his purpose. He doesn't *need* us at all. When we failed in the garden, he could have called it quits. But he takes delight in us. He *wants* to bless us. He *wants* to expand our impact. He *wants* to help us grow. He *wants* to build relationship with us. But it takes action on our part to walk with him, no matter the cost. Unlocking your purpose is a continual process of growing your faith. Some growth looks like subtle, natural decisions, and some make you hold your breath. But all of them draw us closer to the Father, and farther into the purpose he has for our lives.

What do you feel God guiding you to change about your day-to-day life to better represent your status as a Child of God?

Something I've noticed over my years of following Christ is that he doesn't call out all of our faults at once. (Whew! I'm so grateful!) That is good news because we're not overwhelmed right away when we say yes to following Jesus. But it also requires consistent self-inventory because it's a process that never stops.

I knew when I started following Jesus that drugs and alcohol didn't belong in the picture. (We're not getting into a conversation about alcohol here. This is a personal conviction I had right from the start.) But God didn't point out everything at once. He didn't convict me of the way I was dressing on that same day. He didn't bring up the music I was listening to until much later. And it was even further down the road that I started to feel a check in my spirit about the crime shows I used to love. That's the beauty of walking with Jesus. He's gracious, patient, and personal. He works uniquely in each of us, not through a one-size-fits-all list of rules, but through relationship. As we keep listening, keep growing, and keep stepping forward in faith, He gently reveals what's next. The specifics will look different for all of us, but the invitation is the same: stay aware, stay surrendered, and let him lead.

Every single day, you're presented with situations where you exercise your faith. Whether you take note of them or not. When you stand up for what you believe. When you decide to stay out of a situation that might be compromising, even though all of your friends are going. When you choose to speak the truth. When you put a stop to a conversation filled with gossip. You either respond with faith in God or you respond out of scarcity. We can shy away from acting in faith if we ultimately think it's up to us to have everything figured out. That our success or failure ultimately rests on our own shoulders. Any reason we choose not to exercise our faith is something to wrestle with.

Do we think God is playing a joke on us and is going to call us out on a limb and leave us there?

Is his plan not better than our own?

What is standing in your way right now of walking in bold faith? If God is worth following, isn't he worth trusting?

Our salvation comes completely from the sacrifice Jesus made on the cross. There are no works that can make that more or less solid. Nothing we can do can make us deserve it any more (or less) than we do. We will never earn it or deserve it, but are able to receive it because of the grace and mercy of God. (Ephesians

2:8-9) But we are still called to *demonstrate* our faith through our actions.

FAITH AS A CONCEPT VS. FAITH AS A LIFESTYLE

If God is worth following, isn't he worth trusting?

There is a difference between saying you have faith and demonstrating that faith through your lifestyle. The Bible tells us that it is impossible to please God without faith (Hebrews 11:6). It also tells us that faith is not passive. It requires movement.

> What good is it, dear brothers and sisters, if you say you have faith but don't show it by your actions? Can that kind of faith save anyone?
> James 2:14

It's much easier to say you have faith than to walk it out in real-life situations. But faith isn't a theory. Faith isn't a religious checkbox. It's the difference maker when it comes to walking in your complete purpose or playing small. Where do we hesitate when God calls us forward? Career changes that don't make sense on paper? Forgiving when it feels impossible? Saying yes to leadership when self-doubt is screaming "Imposter! Imposter!"? Taking a financial risk in obedience to God? Writing a book when you know there are a million people better qualified?

Our faith is tested and stretched in real-life situations, and we have the choice to say yes, even when those things don't exactly make sense, or to say no, stay still, and miss all that God wants to unlock in our life. I picture our purpose in Christ like a video game. Which is weird because I never play video games. But my son loves them! (He gets that from his dad.) He loves to show me all of the things, and I usually hear running commentary coming from the other room when he's playing. Based on what I've observed, this seems like the perfect way to envision taking the next step of faith.

When you're on a level in most games, whether you like the level you're on or not, you often can't get to the next level without some task or completion. You don't just get to decide to level up. But man, when you do! A new world opens up! New challenges, new backgrounds, sometimes new outfits (I'm here for that). It's a whole new world! New things to discover. But you didn't get there just because you felt like it. You had to battle or work through what came before. And now that you're here, you're going to battle or work again until you get to what's next. Yes, there will be trials as we walk in faith. But those trials are never in vain. James 1:3 tells us that those trials that test our faith are what produce endurance in us! So consider it joy!

> So be truly glad. There is wonderful joy ahead, even though you must endure many trials for a little while. These trials will show that your faith is genuine. It is being tested as fire tests and purifies gold—though your faith is far more precious than mere gold. So when your faith remains strong through many trials, it will bring you much praise and glory and honor on the day when Jesus Christ is revealed to the whole world. You love him even though you have never seen

him. Though you do not see him now, you trust
him; and you rejoice with a glorious, inexpressible
joy. The reward for trusting him will be the
salvation of your souls.
1 Peter 1:6-9

The beauty of allowing endurance to grow, walking through trials
and periods of refining, is that there is always something new to
discover. There is always more growth around the corner. If we
keep taking the next right step, we will keep hearing "New Level
Unlocked!" It's in the testing of your faith, or putting your faith
into action, that it is proven genuine. There is a lot of talk about
refining and pruning in the Bible. Neither of these processes is fun.
It's the burning of a metal that purifies or refines it, and it's the
cutting of a tree or plant that produces growth. Both processes put
the metal or plant through strain, stress, and loss. We'll reference
the pruning of plants here because that's a subject I know well. For
a plant to grow to its full capacity, sometimes you have to prune it.
Cut away and remove what is holding the plant back from
flourishing.

I've had to make some painful cuts in my years of plant
keeping. I've had plants that were growing so well, looking
amazing, then I made a mistake. I neglected water in a dry season,
or I ignored a lighting change. Something happened that
compromised the health of the plant. Well, now you have an
incredible plant you love that has a portion that is not healthy at
all. While I stare at it and think, I can't believe I'm going to have
to cut all of that off to make the plant healthy again, you can't get
around the pruning process if you want to continue to grow a
flourishing plant.

Faith as a concept says, 'I know that's the next right move, but it will be okay. I'll give it some extra fertilizer or something.' Faith as a lifestyle says, I know that's the next right move, I'm nervous, but I know it has to happen–make the cut. So I make the cut. I mourn the loss. Then I take a little extra care of it for a while while it adjusts to its new life without that section of the plant. Because faith = action even when it's hard. There's a reason there are so many plant references in the Bible. This is verbatim what we have to do in our lives to truly walk in radical obedience, on mission with God, demonstrating our faith in action.

You may have to look at a relationship and think, "I don't know what life will look like without you in it, but you're hindering my growth." You may have to look at a habit or hangup you have and say, "Enough is enough. God has given me the power of self-control, and I choose growth and purpose over this thing that is keeping me from flourishing."

What needs to be pruned from your life for you to flourish and walk in purpose the way God intended? It's likely something you don't want to admit. It's likely something you'll need to mourn for a time. But just like a plant will flourish when you cut off what is holding it back, so will you. Faith is stepping out before the whole picture is in focus. There is often risk. Yes. There is often a cost. But what is the cost of standing still?

I am the true grapevine, and my Father is the gardener. He cuts off every branch of mine that doesn't produce fruit, and he prunes the branches that do bear fruit so they will produce even more. You have already been pruned and purified by the

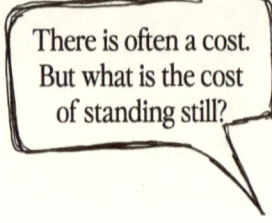

There is often a cost. But what is the cost of standing still?

message I have given you. Remain in me, and I will remain in you. For a branch cannot produce fruit if it is severed from the vine, and you cannot be fruitful unless you remain in me.

Yes, I am the vine; you are the branches. Those who remain in me, and I in them, will produce much fruit. For apart from me you can do nothing. Anyone who does not remain in me is thrown away like a useless branch and withers. Such branches are gathered into a pile to be burned. But if you remain in me and my words remain in you, you may ask for anything you want, and it will be granted! When you produce much fruit, you are my true disciples. This brings great glory to my Father.
John 15:1-8

Do you believe that God has your good in mind? Do you believe that he will fill your life with people who are *for* you when you separate from the ones who aren't? Do you believe that God will honor your obedience? Do you believe what the Bible says only in theory, or are you willing to walk it out by making the hard decision?

Regardless of what might cause us to hesitate to obey, God has already given us all we need to walk firmly in confidence through the pruning process.

For God has not given us a spirit of fear and timidity, but of power, love, and self-discipline.

2 Timothy 1:7

Write this scripture somewhere you will see it and remember–it's not that you won't feel the fear, but it has no power over you. Put fear aside as you take that next step forward.

What if your next step of faith will reach farther than you could imagine?

FAITH OVER FEAR

Faith is one of the most uncomfortable things about living an impactful life. Faith, by definition, will always have risk involved because you can't prove or define what you're doing. The full finished picture isn't in focus for you, so you certainly can't explain it to anyone else.

Just as Abraham wasn't going to be able to explain what he was heading to do to Isaac, sometimes we're called to take steps of faith (not like THAT, thankfully!) that are hard to explain to other people. Sometimes, even to yourself! You can know that God has called you to do something, but it just doesn't make sense on paper. That can leave you feeling alone at times.

I have found that the people who are the very closest to you (I'm talking 2-3 people) will be good sources of encouragement. If they're the right people, that is. (See the section above about pruning the wrong ones!) But even the people who you feel *should* get it might not.

This is when it's a great time to remember Mary's decision on how to handle a world of overwhelming truths and thoughts. God was calling her to carry, give birth to, and raise the Son of

113

God. Scripture tells us that after all she had been through leading up to the birth of Jesus, shepherds came to worship him and told them of the angels coming to announce his birth. That's an overwhelming birth story! But "Mary kept all these things in her heart and thought about them often." (Luke 2:19)

Sometimes that's just the right move. Sometimes what the Lord has spoken to you, or called you to do, isn't for everyone else at the moment. Be ok with holding those things close, moving in the direction God has called you, and talking about the full story when it feels like the right time.

If you haven't noticed, the majority of people out there aren't making the decisions necessary to unlock new levels in their life with Christ. It can be sad to realize that there is no favor from the Lord that is withheld from anyone. The difference maker is who says yes to his calling without hesitation, and who loves their own life on their own terms too much to do the hard things.

Not everyone will understand the radical obedience required to walk in radical faith, even those closest to you. But radical obedience isn't about everyone understanding. It's about trusting God's voice above all else. When you feel afraid to say yes to the picture that isn't entirely in focus yet, remember that God is *for* you.

> So be strong and courageous! Do not be afraid and
> do not panic before them. For the Lord your God
> will personally go ahead of you. He will neither
> fail you nor abandon you.
> Deuteronomy 31:6

Where is God asking you to step forward in faith?

What excuses or fears are keeping you from saying yes?

If you knew the outcome was secure in God's hands, what would you do differently today?

Write down one area where you've hesitated to act in faith. Now, what's one step you can take today? Call someone. Make the decision. Say the yes. Your next step of faith could reach farther than you imagine.

05
OBEDIENCE > FEELINGS

Obedience. (Shudder) That word sounds so overbearing. Obedience is a word that immediately gives off a stifling feeling. You are supposed to obey your parents. Obey teachers. Obey the law. It is usually the rules we follow so we don't get in trouble. And that's exactly what the word means. It's submitting to someone else's authority. But as we often find in the Kingdom of God, obedience to the Lord is upside down from the way we generally associate it with our natural relationships.

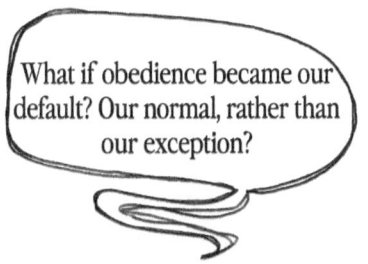

Obedience is often seen as the hard choice, the bold step, the thing we do when we're feeling particularly strong or spiritual. But what if obedience became our default? Our normal, rather than our exception? And what if (gasp) it wasn't a struggle, but second nature? What if we didn't only obey in the big, dramatic moments, but practiced it so regularly in our daily lives that when the big moments came, we were already prepared?

Jesus knew scripture as well (better) as anyone. And he could sum up all of the law into two commandments: love God and love people. If you operate out of love, you're constantly thinking about the good of the other. The greatest commandment we're given as Christ followers is to love the Lord with all your heart and with all your soul and with all your mind (Matthew 22:37). Ok, love. That sounds great. What a great God.

How do we show him love?

If you love me, obey my commandments.
John 14:15

Even further…

Loving God means keeping his commandments, and his commandments are not burdensome.
1 John 5:3

So we show love through obedience. But not burdensome? There is a whole Bible of instruction and commands! How could that not be burdensome? That's the question. And there lies the heart of this chapter. In a friendship, relationship, or even a parent/child relationship, none will survive if one person is always just looking out for themselves. There is an entire chapter of the Bible dedicated to what love is, just so there is no confusion. And there is no bit about it being all about you.

Love is patient and kind. Love is not jealous or boastful or proud or rude. It does not demand its own way. It is not irritable, and it keeps no record of being wronged. It does not rejoice about injustice but rejoices whenever the truth wins out. Love never gives up, never loses faith, is always hopeful, and endures through every circumstance.
1 Corinthians 13:4-7

This is our love for God, and this is our love for each other. But even that sounds burdensome, right? Not if it's genuine love. I love my child, so you don't have to convince me to practice these qualities of love. Am I perfect at all of them every day? Not by a long shot. But when caught in the moment, I can see where I've missed it and wish I had done better, then I aim for that. I love my husband, and the same is true with him. It's not that I'm never irritable (Rarely, of course. Ha!), but when I realize I'm being irritable, I'm quick to make sure he knows it's not his fault and apologize for the nonsense I'm putting out there. Why? Because it's genuine love. Give yourself some grace here. It doesn't say that love is perfect. But love will always be chasing the best for the other.

How does this relate to our obedience conversation? Well, when you have a genuine love for the Father, it becomes second nature to obey his commands. Most of what he asks of us doesn't feel like a big ask anymore. I spent a lot of time learning about religion and the rules of it all before I truly met Jesus and fell in love with a Savior. Relationship changes everything. Out of love, I can submit and be happy to do so. Out of religious obligation, I saw it as a pass or fail scenario with a God just waiting for me to screw up.

The Living God of the Bible is not that God. He is after restoration with us. He is after relationship with us. To get back to the closeness of Eden. We're not in Eden right now, are we? So he's still pursuing us. Obedience isn't about earning our place with God, or even earning his love. That is unconditional. But sometimes his promises have conditions.

Because we're not living in the perfection of Eden, there's a real tension we all feel: we love the Lord and genuinely want to obey him, but the pull of a fallen world also surrounds us. We are often carrying thoughts, desires, and emotions that don't naturally align with God's will. As someone who's always been a rule follower, I've sometimes wished obedience were just black and white. Clear-cut commands with obvious lines. But God isn't after robotic compliance. He's after real, wholehearted devotion. Obedience that comes from love, not force. He doesn't want a world full of programmed people; He wants sons and daughters who choose him freely.

He has put the ball in our court, and the choice is up to us. Daily.

> This command I am giving you today is not too
> difficult for you, and it is not beyond your reach. It
> is not kept in heaven, so distant that you must ask,
> 'Who will go up to heaven and bring it down so
> we can hear it and obey?' It is not kept beyond the
> sea, so far away that you must ask, 'Who will
> cross the sea to bring it to us so we can hear it and
> obey?' No, the message is very close at hand; it is

on your lips and in your heart so that you can obey it.

Now listen! Today I am giving you a choice between life and death, between prosperity and disaster. For I command you this day to love the Lord your God and to keep his commands, decrees, and regulations by walking in his ways. If you do this, you will live and multiply, and the Lord your God will bless you and the land you are about to enter and occupy.

But if your heart turns away and you refuse to listen, and if you are drawn away to serve and worship other gods, then I warn you now that you will certainly be destroyed. You will not live a long, good life in the land you are crossing the Jordan to occupy.

Today I have given you the choice between life and death, between blessings and curses. Now I call on heaven and earth to witness the choice you make. Oh, that you would choose life, so that you and your descendants might live! You can make this choice by loving the Lord your God, obeying him, and committing yourself firmly to him. This is the key to your life. And if you love and obey the Lord, you will live long in the land the Lord swore to give your ancestors Abraham, Isaac, and Jacob.

Deuteronomy 30:11-20

It's a daily choice that we have to make, but it's ours to make. And the degree to which we cling to obedience and walk closely with Jesus is the degree to which we see our purpose come to life. If we're diligent with the small daily decisions, when big situations arise, we're ready. We already have a foundation built for how we will respond. Our response in a big moment is built on the backbone of "this is what I always do."

HABITUAL OBEDIENCE

My favorite moments in scripture are those that involve people walking through a difficult circumstance, and we see that "they did as they always do." Daniel and Jesus are the ones who come to mind for me. Despite the surroundings and circumstances, they obeyed in the face of fear, pain, and threats. Because of this, power, strength, and provision were granted.

Just as people in the Bible were confronted with impossible circumstances and were able to make good (but hard) decisions, we can do the same. Just like them, we have to be willing to fight our feelings. To row against the current of our nature so that we reach the ultimate destination God has for us. It's never easy to fight your nature. To fight the carnal feelings and desires we have as humans. But when we love and trust God, we can fight the fight knowing what lies on the other side is so much greater than what we could gain through any strength of our own.

Let's look at how Daniel and Jesus responded to some difficult situations in their lives. And by "difficult," I mean the kind of situations that would make the modern-day human down a bottle of Prozac and hide under a blanket.

DANIEL

Like many people we see in the Bible who follow the Lord faithfully, Daniel was given numerous promotions, gifts, and praise during his time in service to the king. But with that comes the people who would love nothing more than to see you fail so they can gain the upper hand. Well, for Daniel, some guys who were jealous of his position were scheming ways to take him down. Daniel 6 says that "they couldn't find anything to condemn. He was faithful, always responsible, and completely trustworthy. So they concluded, 'Our only chance of finding grounds for accusing Daniel will be in connection with the rules of his religion.'" (Daniel 6:4-5)

So they convinced the king to sign a law stating that for 30 days, anyone who prayed to anyone other than the king would be thrown into a den of lions. Not to relax, of course, but to be eaten. That's quite a target.

> But when Daniel learned that the law had been signed, he went home and knelt down *as usual* in his upstairs room, with its windows open toward Jerusalem. He prayed three times a day, *just as he had always done*, giving thanks to his God.
> Daniel 6:10

To save himself, he would have to compromise his integrity and his relationship with God. But he had walked in faithfulness all along, so it wasn't a question. When things got weird, who else would he go to if not God, like he's done all along? Daniel didn't have to strain to be bold in crisis. He already had an established pattern of faithfulness.

So he prayed as he had always done. And that boy didn't get eaten, but did get to relax with those lions. God sent an angel to shut the mouths of the lions, and Daniel walked out without a scratch on him "for he had trusted God." (Daniel 6:23)

This well-known trip to the lion's den wasn't the result of a sudden surge of courage. It was the fruit of a faithful life. Daniel didn't wake up one day and decide to be bold. He simply kept doing what he had always done. Because Daniel obeyed, the king decreed that everyone should worship the true living God! Because Daniel obeyed, he prospered.

Likewise, we don't become obedient in crisis unless we've practiced it in the quiet. Obedience becomes a natural response when it's been rehearsed in daily decisions. Faithfulness in the mundane builds spiritual reflexes. Daniel didn't need to summon courage in the moment. He had built it over time.

We have another example to look at. One whose life was marked by habitual obedience.

JESUS

I know, I know. Jesus is literally the Son of God. He's the only perfect human ever. So that's a lot to live up to. But he was also set as our guide. The Bible tells us that there's not one temptation that Jesus wasn't confronted with while on earth. Fully God, fully man, and fully living out the human experience, even though in an instant he could have called it quits and gone back home.

> This High Priest of ours understands our weaknesses, for he faced all of the same testings we do, yet he did not sin.
> Hebrews 4:15

So let's look at Jesus in a moment where everything could have gone all wrong. In a moment where the humanity of Jesus was pulling double duty against the divine. Jesus was about to be betrayed. He already knew that. And instead of waiting around for the fatal moment, or going to wallow in self-pity for his final moments of freedom, he fell back on a lifetime of obedience and responded *as usual*.

> Then, accompanied by the disciples, Jesus left the upstairs room and went *as usual* to the Mount of Olives. There he told them, "Pray that you will not give in to temptation." He walked away, about a stone's throw, and knelt down and prayed, "Father, if you are willing, please take this cup of suffering away from me. Yet I want your will to be done, not mine." Then an angel from heaven appeared and strengthened him. He prayed more fervently, and he was in such agony of spirit that his sweat fell to the ground like great drops of blood.
> Luke 22:39-44

Jesus' feelings were telling him a lot of things that night. His anxiety was off the charts. We know this not just because, of course, it would be (!!), but because he was sweating blood. He was experiencing a rare condition called hematohidrosis, where, due to stress and anxiety, the blood vessels burst and release blood into the sweat glands. His actual body was revolting.

The feelings of betrayal had to have been overwhelming. A close friend that has followed him and studied under his teachings was about to turn him over for his death. The friends that he wanted to pray with him were falling asleep as if he hadn't been telling them what was about to happen. Oh, and he also already knew every gruesome detail of what lay ahead of him.

He was weak but stayed the course. He could have, in this moment, let his humanity overtake him. He could have said, never mind. No can do. And we would be goners. There would be no redemption through Jesus as we know it. But he chose to buckle down and pray more fervently. Ultimately, he obeyed his calling to death.

> He humbled himself in obedience to God and died
> a criminal's death on a cross.
> Philippians 2:8

With all the stress, emotion, and pressure involved, he chose obedience because it was what he had always done. It's how he lived his life to that point, so it wasn't a question, even in the face of ultimate turmoil. His feelings were real, and he acknowledged them. But he didn't follow them. He followed the Father.

That's the difference. Obedience doesn't require the absence of emotion; it requires the submission of emotion. You can feel fear, grief, anger, or uncertainty and still obey. Obedience that costs us our comfort is often the most powerful. We don't have to wait for our feelings to align before we say yes to God. We have to trust that his will is better than our emotions in the moment.

We live in a culture that would convince us to put a lot of value on our feelings. We're told to follow our hearts, appease our emotions, and avoid anything that feels like self-denial. But the truth is, emotions are meant to be indicators, not dictators. They can inform us, but they were never meant to lead us. We were not designed to live from emotion, but from our identity in Christ.

Fortunately, we'll not have to make that decision with the weight of the future of all mankind on our shoulders. But if you were walking through this moment of Jesus's life, where would you have to tap out? Would it be because of the betrayal? Would it be because of the pain?

Let's make the question feel a little more reasonable. What if you were walking through Daniel's story? Would you be able to continue in obedience despite threats, or would you fold out of fear?

Our emotions will tell us a lot of things. And they're worth paying attention to. But they're not necessarily the best to base your journey on.

EMOTIONS VS. IDENTITY

> We were not designed to live from emotion, but from identity.

Both Daniel and Jesus had emotions. Throughout Jesus' entire ministry, and especially during his journey to the cross, we see very strong emotions. But those emotions were never able to sway who he was. We see him express them. We see him let them have a moment. But they are never able to change his course.

One moment of Jesus's emotions that I love to take note of is when his friend Lazarus died. Jesus knew that he was going to raise him from the dead. He went there knowing that was going to be the outcome. But instead of skipping through the moment, he was present with his friends who were mourning. His good friend was dead. And had been for 4 days. Jesus wept. It even says that anger welled up within him and he was deeply troubled. Jesus felt. Then he stood up and went on to carry out his business. He raised his friend from the dead.

Jesus was fully divine, but his fully human side didn't leave him exempt from emotional wrestling. We see him wrestle, and yet he still chooses obedience every time. In this situation, we even see him place value on the emotions of that moment by not pushing them aside for the task of resurrection. Who wouldn't want to skip ahead to the happy ending? But he allowed himself to be present and feel. In that, we find our permission to acknowledge and express our feelings. To wrestle with our emotions, and still not be ruled by them.

Emotions tell us something about ourselves. They tell us what is going on around us. They're something to take note of. Maybe it's a feeling of discernment. Maybe it is grief. Maybe it is radical joy! They are always worth noting, then discerning. When it comes to obedience, the response may sometimes be, "I don't feel like it." "Why should I obey if I don't feel like doing that? Shouldn't I be true to myself? Authentic to who I am?" Valid question. My return question would be, which self are you being authentic to? We have an old self that should be put away, and we should be living like we're born again. New self.

Since you have heard about Jesus and have learned the truth that comes from him, *throw off* your old sinful nature and your former way of life,

which is corrupted by lust and deception. Instead,
let the Spirit renew your thoughts and attitudes.
Put on your new nature, created to be like God—
truly righteous and holy.
Ephesians 4:21-24

Our old self and new self don't co-exist. We are to discard who we used to be and let the Holy Spirit transform us every day to be more like Jesus. This means that our tendencies, personalities, or even past patterns of disobedience don't get to define us. Maybe you've said, "I'm just not a disciplined person," or "I always struggle with consistency." That may have been true of the old you. But the new you, the one united with Christ, is empowered by the Holy Spirit to walk in obedience.

Before the reality of how heavy that is sinks in, take the weight off. He doesn't say *you* do this. *You* overcome your old self and figure out how to make good decisions through your feelings and emotions. It's his work. Our work is to come to him and allow him to do the work. You're not trying to become obedient through willpower; you're learning to live from who you already are in Christ.

This is a critical shift. When we think we're fighting against ourselves to obey, it becomes exhausting. But when we realize obedience is agreeing with our new nature, it becomes empowering. You're not working to earn righteousness; you're walking in the righteousness that's already been given to you.

Don't copy the behavior and customs of this
world, but let God transform you into a new

person by changing the way you think. Then you
will learn to know God's will for you, which is
good and pleasing and perfect.
Romans 12:2

The beauty of it all is that he will indeed answer us when we pray
for him to change the way we think. It still takes active decision-
making on our part. It still takes daily renewal. But he will help us
through. I love watching a new believer figure it all out. It's a
reminder of when I started following Jesus. No one is perfect right
off the bat. In fact, if someone tells you they've got it all together,
even after years and years of walking with Jesus, run.

I remember after I started following Jesus, I went to a
college worship night with my friend at the time, now husband,
Brandon. (Swoon.) I had changed my heart. I had changed my
phone number. I had changed many things. But I hadn't changed
my wardrobe yet. I was just so excited to be there that I didn't even
notice any of this happening, but Brandon told me later that he
could see people judging me and staring because of what I was
wearing. He said that he just wanted to get in all of their faces and
say, "You don't know what's in there! I can see what she's going to
be." That moment marked me forever. To this day, I enjoy the
process of seeing someone transformed. I never feel the pressure to
force the next step on them, but watch like a flower opening up.
Wait, guys, it's not done. Ok, look now! God is gentle in the
transformation process, and his church should be the same.

For anyone worried about me, I soon realized that I needed
to dress more modestly, and I did. But it didn't come from the
judgment of humans; it came from the gentle transformation of my
thinking by the Lord.

God will continue to transform you as you ask him to. And he is so amazing in that he's not going to throw a laundry list at you all at once. I can't imagine keeping my excitement about following Jesus for very long if I had been met with a list of rules and judgmental faces based on how well I fit in. God planted me in the midst of people who allowed me to grow. Instead of rushing me, they allowed God to gently change my heart day by day. So today I'm just as excited about following him as day one. Only I understand more of his heart, am walking in more of my purpose, and am so passionate to see the local church be that good soil for every person that would follow Jesus.

Side note here for anyone that thinks like me—I was very nervous about being in church again. What I knew in the past turned me into a brainwashed version of myself that was molded to look a certain way. Away from the church I had found more of my genuine self and didn't want to go back. But I can tell you that after 17 years of following Jesus at the time of writing this, the bit of me that I had discovered before Jesus has blossomed into more and more of who I was created to be. In a healthy church and community, the same will happen for you. God created you uniquely and isn't here to squash your personality or your dreams. He's here to help you light it all up and walk in it fully. And contrary to what it would seem when you look at the wrong examples, the best of you is all set free when we walk in obedience. New level unlocked.

Little by little. Day by day. We keep drawing a little closer. You'll have seasons of intense growth, and seasons where it seems a little slower. But we need all of the rhythms in life. If we daily remember that the old self is gone and walk in our new self, we can experience emotions and feelings and learn to work with them in the way God has called us to.

THROW OUT PLAN B

The place where obedience gets tricky is where most things get tricky, when the struggle comes. When everything hits the fan and we're facing a decision. Do I do what I know is the right thing but feels bad in the moment, or the thing that feels easier in the moment that I know isn't the right decision? Or, quite simply, am I going to trust God in this?

If you can't see yourself in the hardest moment possible and know what you would decide, you'll take the easy way out. You have to have a clear plan A with no plan B. Or in the words of Arnold Swarzaneger, "Forget plan B. To test yourself and grow, you have to operate without a safety net." (Please tell me you read that with an accent.) If you have a plan B, you WILL take it.

Through making the small decisions every day to obey, like we've talked about, you do have a foundation to stand on when the hard things come. And they will come. No great thing comes about without sacrifice. Maybe it will be the moment that you have to release a relationship that isn't healthy for you. Maybe it will be the moment you feel betrayed by a friend. Maybe it will be the moment when your spouse or child walks away from faith. Maybe it will be the moment you have to make a difficult career decision. There will be many difficult moments we walk through in life that will cause us to rely on God, because we're not built to carry the weight on our own.

Will you be able to do as you've always done?

Will you be able to obey?

There will be many moments in our lives where we will have to lean on Jesus and trust his Word with every fiber of our being. It's hard to make the difficult decision to obey when we can't see the end results. We feel certain in a decision when there is a calculated outcome. But what I see in scripture is the very opposite of our natural way of thinking.

- The Levites stepped into the Jordan River with the ark, THEN the waters split. (Joshua 3)
- Moses had to put himself out there, and THEN God showed up with miracles and freedom.
- Noah had to build the ark and TRUST that the whole entire earth was really going to flood. (Can you imagine?)

We tend to be people who want certainty, clarity, and full understanding before we move or trust. But God doesn't promise to provide those answers every time. I see that the reward is often on the other side of obedience. There is a lot of promise and potential tied to trusting the Lord and simply taking the steps. One after the other. Extraordinary purpose requires radical obedience.

> I pray that God, the source of hope, will fill you completely with joy and peace because you trust in him. Then you will overflow with confident hope through the power of the Holy Spirit.
> Romans 15:13

We show our love through our obedience. And God reciprocates by continuing to be present and be our strength *because we trust* him. Every act of obedience, no matter how small, is forming you. You are becoming someone whose default is to say yes to God. And when the hard moments come (and they will), you won't be scrambling to find courage. You'll be drawing from a well you've already been filling.

TAKE INVENTORY

What does daily obedience look like for you? Do you have a pattern of compromise when things get hard? Do

> Every act of obedience, no matter how small, is forming you.

you give up when you have a bump in the road? Or do you press on knowing that the little things have the power to take you out if you're not dead set on fulfilling the calling God has placed on your life?

One of my mentors taught me the principle of duty, discipline, and delight, and it has stuck with me. I want to share it with you. It will be life-changing if you recognize how simple but true this process is.

With any form of obedience, it may start out as a duty. The Bible says to read the Word, so I start a reading plan. I don't always feel like it, but I do it out of duty to what God has said. If you remain diligent in that duty, you'll realize it has become a discipline. Meaning, it's no longer something you force yourself to do out of obligation, but it's a discipline in your life. Something you do regularly because you recognize that it is good for your life. You recognize the benefit of making it a habit. As you keep practicing it as a discipline, before you know it, you're taking delight in the same thing you once did out of obligation. You find joy in it. You find life in it. And you can't imagine removing it from your life.

This principle is true of developing a prayer life, of working out, of tithing, you name it. I know you've heard it said way too many times, but if it were easy, everyone would do it. It takes making a decision and walking it out.

So, how do you love God? Will you be able to set your feelings aside and obey? Not obey some, but obey all?

Walking in purpose calls for radical obedience. You're telling me that to be great, this is the first step? What a boring answer! It would almost seem easier if the answer were to go get some special Bible degree or go on some freaky retreat where all of the answers will be revealed. No. Even the most extraordinary thing you can dream of starts here, with obedience. We often look for one huge answer to our purpose without realizing that the answer is the sum of every step we take when we take them with the Lord. You have to cultivate daily faithfulness so that radical obedience becomes natural.

This is your invitation to live from who you are in Christ, not how you feel today. Obedience isn't about mustering up strength; it's about trusting the one who made you new. Let your yes come from your identity, not your mood. And as you walk in daily obedience, you'll find that radical obedience is no longer rare. It's just who you are.

06
COMFORT KILLS

There's something about stepping into uncharted waters that feels scary. It can feel like a lake to me. The water is murky and, depending on which lake it is, possibly just gross. I do not like a lake. I like to sit on a dock and look at a lake. I like to sip coffee while staring at a lake. I even like riding in a boat across a lake and taking it all in. But nothing is beckoning me to get into a lake. It seems like the things nightmares are made of. Bottoms you can't see. Mud that sucks you in. Slimy surfaces and weird fish, and dead bodies. No, thank you.

But sometimes a plunge into the unknown is the exact right next step to reach the reward on the other side.

Comfort zones feel like a really safe and cozy place to be. It's called the comfort zone for a reason! But when we overstay our welcome, a comfort zone can become a prison. And one we're not likely to try to break out of. Especially the longer we're there.

Now, relax a little. We're not called to be uncomfortable in every single moment. But comfort isn't the goal. Obedience is.

Growth isn't comfortable. Plants grow best when they're pruned. Muscles have to be torn to grow. Even career growth requires stretching. You don't wake up and find yourself living the dream. You have to make the decisions along the way that take you from where you are to the next step forward. Sometimes those steps will be easy, and sometimes they will be really difficult. But if you never take a step past what you know, you'll settle for the life you know right now. What could you be leaving on the table if you don't move?

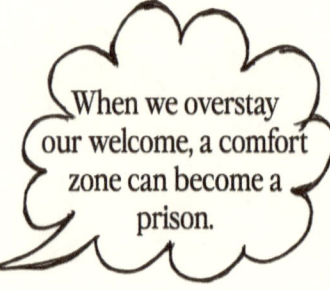

When we overstay our welcome, a comfort zone can become a prison.

Think back to Jesus calling the 12 disciples. He called them to walk away from everything that had shaped them up to that point. They walked away from their work, from their families, from their routine, all so they could be discipled by Jesus. I must think that, given the strong personalities the disciples seemed to have, one of them would have let us know if Jesus had called someone who declined the invitation. It probably would have been John. He felt it noteworthy to record for all time that he runs faster than Peter, so I guarantee he would have noted that invite number 13 was declined, and pointing and laughing were involved.

The 12 knew that an invitation from Jesus was important. And they dropped everything to follow. When we get the call, will we be ready to put obedience over preference? I received a call once that flew me way past my comfort zone, and it was one of the scariest yeses I've given.

WORK WITH...WOMEN??

When I was growing up, all I observed of a ministry for women was covered in flowers and doilies. You know, those things that are lacy and you'd only find them a home belonging to someone quite old, sitting under the dish of hard candies that are all stuck together. You can probably smell powdery perfume and see the floral couch in your mind if you know what I'm talking about.

Besides that not being an aesthetic I was ready to identify with, that visual was accompanied by Bible studies with no depth, and women who were merely going to be pleasant church company, and no deeper. If you don't know what I mean by that, good. It's a nice way of saying the conversation was the kind that stopped short of life-changing, and certainly didn't approach iron sharpening iron. Now layer onto that the fact that I've always been a tomboy and preferred the company of guys over gals. Women's ministry just wasn't something I envisioned in my future.

When I knew there was a stir in my heart to start a women's ministry at our church, I was a little more than put off by the thought. I had a conversation with my best friend that I do ministry alongside, and she felt the same stir AND had the same reaction. No. Way.

I'm a worship leader. I'm a graphic designer. I'm not a women's ministry person!

Women are catty. They're back biters. They tear each other down to make themselves feel better. They would run over another woman to get a better position. They gossip and are rude and stuck-up. ... Hey Jen, that's why they need you. Ok, God. Let me pray about it. Oh, wait.

After a couple of years of praying that he would change his mind, my friend and I, in the same season, realized that God was saying it was time. It took all of the faith we could muster to step up to lead the women of our church, but what God did as we took that plunge into the unknown was breathtaking. (And not in a drowning kind of way like we feared.)

He revealed the passion that he had been growing in us all along. He gave us a soft spot for women to find more than they had known in their walk with the Lord. And even more, he put weight on our hearts for the women in the areas surrounding our city as well. Danielle and I moved into building community with women through small groups. Then gathering women and pastoring them. Then, hosting a podcast as a way to disciple women. Not only did we not die when we jumped out of our comfort zone, but we have also been able to witness a beautiful movement in women. There is still a lot of change to be had, but we are able to gather in a community of women who aren't backbiting. They're not catty. They're beautiful. They want the best for each other. And they pray for every woman around them to find the same thing.

It's been a win for women, a win for our church, and a win for Danielle and me. He has grown us in ways we would have never imagined while we were sitting cozy on the dock, looking out over the unknown. The scary part is that we could have stayed there and never known what we were missing.

What is just on the other side of the plunge for you? You'll never know if you don't jump.

THE CALL THAT DISRUPTS COMFORT

Remember Abraham?

The Lord had said to Abram, "Leave your native country, your relatives, and your father's family, and go to the land that I will show you. I will make you into a great nation. I will bless you and make you famous, and you will be a blessing to others. I will bless those who bless you and curse those who treat you with contempt. All the families on earth will be blessed through you." So Abram departed as the Lord had instructed, and Lot went with him. Abram was seventy-five years old when he left Haran.
Genesis 12:1-4

He was called to take quite a plunge. God asked him to leave everything, travel to an undisclosed destination, and, oh yeah, have a baby, even though they were way too old to have babies. Without hesitation, Abraham packed up his 75-year-old self, family, and belongings and headed out. Talk about a wing and a prayer! As they headed out to their yet-to-be-revealed secret destination, God kept confirming his calling. He made a covenant with Abraham. The scripture even says that "God counted him as righteous because of his faith" (Genesis 15:6). God walked with Abraham in such an intimate way as he kept saying yes to God, despite how ambiguous the whole thing felt.

Because Abraham chose obedience over what he knew—over the comfort of his native land, his family, and friends–the whole trajectory of history was changed. All the way down the family tree to us today. Obedience often comes without the full picture in view, but the reward is on the other side.

We've visited this story before. But we've not looked at little nephew who was tagging along. Lot's dad died, so he was hanging with Abraham's family on the journey. In the process, he became wealthy and prosperous, like Abraham, so the two parted ways to ensure they had enough land for all their animals and tents.

Lot ends up in a famously wicked little town called Sodom. It's so wicked that God is about to rain down fire and wipe it out. But before he does, he has a little chat with Abraham and lets him in on his plan. Abraham tries to go to bat for the righteous people there, but as it turns out, there are none. They're going down. But the Lord sends help to get Lot and his family out before it's destroyed.

Here's where the difference comes in. Abraham consistently obeyed without question. Without hesitation. But not the same for Lot. His yes was shrouded in hesitation. The desire to cling to the life they knew.

> At dawn the next morning the angels became insistent. "Hurry," they said to Lot. "Take your wife and your two daughters who are here. Get out right now, or you will be swept away in the destruction of the city!"
>
> When Lot still hesitated, the angels seized his hand and the hands of his wife and two daughters and rushed them to safety outside the city, for the Lord was merciful. When they were safely out of the city, one of the angels ordered, "Run for your lives! And don't look back or stop

anywhere in the valley! Escape to the mountains, or you will be swept away!"
Genesis 19:15-19

Off they go. But we're not in the clear yet...

Lot reached the village just as the sun was rising over the horizon. Then the Lord rained down fire and burning sulfur from the sky on Sodom and Gomorrah. He utterly destroyed them, along with the other cities and villages of the plain, wiping out all the people and every bit of vegetation. But Lot's wife looked back as she was following behind him, and she turned into a pillar of salt.
Genesis 19:23-26

Hesitation, then flat-out disobedience. And she's a goner. When we take the time to look back on the comforts of a place God has called us out of, we take the breath out of the new life in front of us. As a child, and even now, I try to get a mental picture of a pillar of salt. Naturally, I think of a giant pillar like on the front of the White House made of salt, just sitting there. Like, *poof!* Now you're a pillar of salt kind of moment.

But what's truly interesting about this scripture is that the word for pillar in Hebrew is a garrison or an outpost. A place set for keeping watch over an area. So whatever she physically looked like, whatever happened in that moment, she is turned into this pillar of salt right there by the Dead Sea, where no life exists to this day. Death by disobedience left to watch over a place that can sustain no life. What a sobering warning not to look back or cling to our comfort zones when God has called us to move.

We hear nothing of Lot's wife until this moment, then she's set up as a warning for all time. Jesus references her when asked about his second coming. Don't look back! You've been called to a purpose and a walk that is different from the people around you. Don't fall into the comforts and pressure to fit in. Remember Lot's wife!

> And the world will be as it was in the days of Lot. People went about their daily business—eating and drinking, buying and selling, farming and building— until the morning Lot left Sodom. Then fire and burning sulfur rained down from heaven and destroyed them all. Yes, it will be 'business as usual' right up to the day when the Son of Man is revealed. On that day a person out on the deck of a roof must not go down into the house to pack. A person out in the field must not return home. Remember what happened to Lot's wife! If you cling to your life, you will lose it, and if you let your life go, you will save it.
> Luke 17:28-33

OBEDIENCE INVOLVES RISK

Obedience can often involve risk. Whether it's putting yourself out there emotionally, putting relationships on the line, or risking your reputation, radical obedience often calls us to a different and higher standard than the people around us are willing to live by.

While that risk may appear too costly when we look on the surface, it can all change when we realize who is holding us on the other side.

What if we reframed the way we see obedience that calls us out of our comfort zone? Not as a risk, but as holy ground. What if we could see that it's through the testing that we're made strong, and we welcomed the challenge instead of wrapping up tighter in our blanket? When we step out of our comfort zone, the real work begins. It's in the moments that we know we have to completely rely on the Lord that he can do his best work.

> Each time he said, "My grace is all you need. My
> power works best in weakness." So now I am glad
> to boast about my weaknesses, so that the power
> of Christ can work through me.
> 2 Corinthians 12:9

This sentiment is given many times throughout the Bible. Why would God do something amazing through us or in our lives if it could be attributed to our own strength? When we operate in our weakness, it becomes obvious where the hand of God is at work. When we are forced to admit that we don't have the strength to carry ourselves through a challenge or a growth season, or a heavy season, that's when God reveals himself the most, and transformation happens. Not because he's not present in the good times or the easy times, but because we're probably not paying as much attention.

What are we waiting for when we know that God is faithful?

The Lord directs the steps of the godly.
He delights in every detail of their lives.
Though they stumble, they will never fall,
for the Lord holds them by the hand.
Psalm 37:23-24

What do we have to be afraid of when God is doing the calling AND the catching? If we trust God, we can trust his Word. His Word reveals his character, and his character is consistent. He is always faithful. He is always present. He is always listening and guiding. There are no promises that say walking in the life he has called us to will be easy. But a whole lot of promises that say he will never leave us or forsake us. (Hebrews 13:5) That he will fight for us. (Exodus 14:14) That he will give us strength and peace. (Psalm 29:11)

1 Corinthians 10:12-14 tells us that we will absolutely go through hard things and he's not going to transport us out of them, but show us a way out so that we can endure them. Because he is faithful. God is a good father, and a good father doesn't just make everything magical for his children. He knows that if he does, they will never be able to stand on their own two feet. They'll never develop any resilience. But to stay close in the hard times, watch them stumble, then figure it out. Strength is built.

Think about when the Israelites were wandering through the desert for those 40 years. What a time of trial and frustration. Every bit of provision or devastation depended on their obedience. But, man, the miracles and transformations they witnessed while walking closely with God! He led them as a cloud in the day to shield the sun. He led them as fire at night to light their way. This was a time when the Holy Spirit had not yet come, so to have God with them in a tangible way every single day was incredible! He provided food and water and everything they needed. For 40 years, even their sandals didn't wear out!

When you feel like you're out on a limb and have to trust God for every next step, you'll never grow faster. It can be difficult to appreciate the season when you're in the middle of the struggle, but you'll come to see the sweetness that can be found in being that reliant on the Lord.

When Danielle and I stepped out and started a women's ministry, we had to (and still do) take every single step covered in prayer because we knew that we didn't have it inside of us naturally. We didn't know how to lead women. We hadn't seen this done in a way we could use as a model. We were just gleaning from every good thing we could piece together out there, offering God our best, and praying that he would do the hard part–changing lives.

There was so much pressure to do this well. Not from any outside sources, but from two hearts that just want to honor God. Are we really hearing from God? Is he *sure* we are capable? Will he still be showing us the next right step 6 months from now? 5 years from now? We adore our church and our leadership, and we want everything we put our hands to to reflect the heart of God and the vision of our pastors. I'm just going to say it… There was a lot less to worry about before we said yes! But God has been faithful in every single moment. He consistently offers us Abraham moments of confirmation as we walk to this undisclosed destination with him.

I was a lot more comfortable in my wheelhouse–leading worship and designing cool things. But when I stepped out of that comfort zone, I was able to see something entirely new bloom within me that I would have never known was there if I had taken the easy route.

Are you willing to get uncomfortable?

FAITH REQUIRES MOVEMENT

We are saved by faith. But our faith is shown through our actions. Faith is not just a feeling but a movement. There's a big difference between believing in Jesus and following Jesus. Lip service will get us nowhere. How will we respond when our faith is called into action? Will we shrink back or walk in obedience, just as Jesus walked?

> You say you have faith, for you believe that there is one God. Good for you! Even the demons believe this, and they tremble in terror. How foolish! Can't you see that faith without good deeds is useless?
> James 2:19-20

Sometimes the movement God is asking for can seem trivial, but maybe it's to see how we will respond. Will we be faithful in the small things? Are we ready for the next step? Jesus taught Simon to step out of his comfort zone with a seemingly trivial request.

Simon had been fishing all night long, and he and the other fishermen were on the shore there washing out their nets. Jesus was on the shore preaching, and as usual, the crowds were insane. So he asks Simon if they can get into his boat and go just a little bit from shore so he can preach to the people without being suffocated. Simon agrees to help, and they go sit in the boat.

> When he had finished speaking, he said to Simon, "Now go out where it is deeper, and let down your nets to catch some fish."
>
> "Master," Simon replied, "we worked hard all last night and didn't catch a thing. But if you say so, I'll let the nets down again." And this time their nets were so full of fish they began to tear! A shout for help brought their partners in the other boat, and soon both boats were filled with fish and on the verge of sinking.
>
> When Simon Peter realized what had happened, he fell to his knees before Jesus and said, "Oh, Lord, please leave me—I'm such a sinful man." For he was awestruck by the number of fish they had caught, as were the others with him. His partners, James and John, the sons of Zebedee, were also amazed.
>
> Jesus replied to Simon, "Don't be afraid! From now on you'll be fishing for people!" And as soon as they landed, they left everything and followed Jesus.
> Luke 5:4-11

He started by making excuses, gave in reluctantly, then was amazed at the result. Even reluctant obedience was rewarded! Simon was a fisherman, so we have to assume that he knew what he was talking about. They had fished all night and caught nothing, so I feel like the eye roll that happened here is still echoing to this day. He knew his patterns. He knew the routine. He knew how to catch fish. But sometimes the patterns and routines we create for ourselves can keep us trapped in a comfortable place. These things aren't bad in themselves! We're not meant to live 100% of the time in a frenzy. That's not sustainable. But when it's time to move, it's time to muster your faith and move. God has a much richer life planned for us than what we will experience if we never ask him what is next.

Don't overcomplicate what this plunge looks like in your life. God will ask us to do things that he has already gifted us for. He's not asking us to take a plunge into the unknown with no ability to swim. He's asking you to realize what is already in your hands and trust him with it. God's thinking is far above anything we can know. He sees the ingredients and knows what they can become. We sometimes need to see things in a fresh way that we've always had or always known. Stepping out involves risk because it's unknown, and it will likely cost us something. But we're not going to drown. We have a lifeguard on duty!

> This is my command—be strong and courageous!
> Do not be afraid or discouraged. For the Lord your
> God is with you wherever you go.
> Joshua 1:9

Where are you sitting safely on the dock when God is inviting you into the deep?

STRETCH IT OUT

When we stay safe, we miss out on the opportunities for growth that can arise in our lives. Growth is abandoned in the comfort zone. When I stepped out of my comfort zone into women's ministry, I couldn't imagine an alternate world where I bailed. So many lives have been changed through that community. So many women have found Jesus, felt seen by other women in a positive way for the first time, and been prayed for by people who genuinely cared for them. It's the kind of work that only God can do, but someone had to say yes for it to have a home. I trusted God to do the work, but I have experienced so much growth along the way. That yes came with so many gifts that I didn't see coming.

Danielle and I work better together now than we ever have before because we learned how to truly see and trust the differences that God has brought together between us. Hosting a podcast to disciple women has transformed my ability to prepare content for preaching and even writing for this book. Things I didn't even have on my radar when the shaky yes came out of my mouth. You may have to walk out of the comfort zone trembling, but you can walk knowing it's not resting on your own strength. You can walk knowing that the one who called you is able to see it all through.

Growth is abandoned in the comfort zone.

Fear is the greatest barrier to leaving our comfort zone. It's in those moments where we feel afraid, and we're being stretched more than we can handle, that the best idea is to hit our knees. Prayer is what's called for to gather strength. To realign ourselves with the reality that the Holy Spirit is within us. That God is walking with us. To recognize that "The Spirit of God, who raised Jesus from the dead, lives in you." (Romans 8:11)

> I prayed to the Lord, and he answered me. He freed me from all my fears. Those who look to him for help will be radiant with joy; no shadow of shame will darken their faces.
> Psalm 34:4-5

STEP OFF THE DOCK

"A ship is always safe at the shore-but that is not what it is built for." –Albert Einstein

At the end of the day, you were just meant for more than a mediocre faith or a mediocre life. To settle for less than God's ultimate plan is a heartbreaking reality. You were meant to live fully. To recognize the strength of your voice. To realize the influence you have. What is that thing for you? Don't overthink it or compare someone else's plunge to your own. Your life as a teacher, a business owner, a parent, a doctor, a minister, a student, or any other role you walk in has purpose all over it. We are called to be a body with many parts, and every single part is essential. Even the ones that don't get the same attention as some of the other parts. Don't discount your call, your influence, or your purpose.

Name your dock. What is the comfort zone you're sitting in? What might be on the other side of your obedience? You won't always feel equipped for the next step. You won't always feel ready for the next step. But what will it cost you to say no? What's the worst that can happen if you say yes? What's the best thing that can happen? The lake may still look murky. But what if the real danger isn't in jumping, but in never leaving the dock?

Hold your nose–it's time to jump.

part 3

Embrace the
GREATNESS
God Has For You

PART 3
Embrace the Greatness
God Has For You

Up until now, your yes has been personal. It has cost you comfort, control, and maybe even the approval of others. But radical obedience was never meant to end with you—it was always meant to move through you. This part of your journey is not just about walking in purpose; it's about what your obedience creates, cultivates, and leaves behind. The call of God on your life is never only about your life. It's about the people watching, the ones following, and the generations coming after you. As Psalm 145:4 declares, "Let each generation tell its children of your mighty acts; let them proclaim your power." Your obedience becomes the story they inherit.

In Chapter 7, we'll expose the dangers of playing small. Of shrinking back under the illusion of humility or fear disguised as wisdom. Obedience isn't safe. It's bold. It calls you to step into arenas bigger than your qualifications because that's where God shows off his glory. Then in Chapter 8, we'll confront the price of greatness. There is no legacy without sacrifice. True impact doesn't come from comfort; it comes from consistent, costly obedience that chooses faith over ease. Over and over again. Finally, in Chapter 9, we'll turn our eyes to the baton. How to finish well, multiply what God has given you, and invest your yes in ways that will outlive you.

You don't get to choose whether your life leaves a legacy. You only get to choose what kind.

This part of the book will challenge you to live beyond yourself. To stop measuring your obedience by how it feels, and start measuring it by who it's forming. If the earlier chapters built your foundation, this part is about building forward. For the people you'll never meet, but whose lives will be forever shaped by your faithfulness.

As we move into this part of the book, let these questions stir your thinking as we turn the page:

- Are you more focused on comfort in the present or impact in the future?

- Who is watching your obedience, and what are they learning about God because of it?

- Have you been playing small in areas where God has called you to lead, speak, or build? Why?

- What kind of legacy is your current obedience building?

You don't have to be able to answer these questions fully before we move on, but let your spirit sit with them for a moment. We're about to take off running, and we'll see how your next yes is, indeed, bigger than you think.

07
YOU WERE MADE FOR MORE — ACT LIKE IT

"Understanding the value of something determines how we guard it." —Donna Pisani

There was a moment after Moses died that Joshua had to step up into greatness. Into more. He had been an assistant for a really long time. But now it was time to lead the people of Israel into the reward that God had promised all of those years ago. I can only imagine what was going through Joshua's mind as he realized this tipping point that had come. The Lord said to Joshua,

> For I will be with you as I was with Moses. I will not fail you or abandon you. Be strong and courageous, for you are the one who will lead these people to possess all the land I swore to their

ancestors I would give them. Be strong and very courageous. Be careful to obey all the instructions Moses gave you. Do not deviate from them, turning either to the right or to the left. Then you will be successful in everything you do. Study this Book of Instruction continually. Meditate on it day and night so you will be sure to obey everything written in it. Only then will you prosper and succeed in all you do. This is my command—be strong and courageous! Do not be afraid or discouraged. For the Lord your God is with you wherever you go.

Joshua 1:5b-9

Could God have been clearer? If you follow the steps I've outlined for you, then you will achieve all the success I've promised. I've empowered you, I've called you, I've directed your path to this moment. Will you carry the next steps? Joshua had the choice in that moment to be what he's always been and look for another leader to follow, or he could see the moment that he had been walking towards for years, follow the voice of the Lord, and step into more.

We can become so distracted by our obsession to find one supreme, singular "calling" that we miss how God weaves purpose into every step. No step is insignificant because they all grow us towards the next point God is calling us to. If we miss the value in the process, we can overlook all of the steps that equip us for the big one. The moment when it's time to trust him and take a big step into that very purpose we've been looking for, or may not have even seen coming.

Joshua spotted what the Lord was doing and went out to prepare the people for moving into the promised land. Because this was all the Lord's doing, the people said, "We will do whatever you command us, and we will go wherever you send us. We will obey you just as we obeyed Moses. And may the Lord your God be with you as he was with Moses. Anyone who rebels against your orders and does not obey your words and everything you command will be put to death. So be strong and courageous!" (Joshua 1:16-18)

Playing small and shrinking back has no place in your life with Christ. If God has called you, he has equipped you with all you need to walk it out. Before Joshua's time, Moses responded very differently to a call from the Lord. Remember back in chapter 2? Excuse City. Moses focused on his shortcomings even when the actual Living God was speaking to him, telling him his next steps out loud! I feel like Moses had to have grown in his ability to trust God and lead the people because it wasn't a question for Joshua. Joshua had been under Moses's leadership for a long time and was witness to how God had equipped him in each moment over the years. It was a no-brainer for him to trust the voice of God because he had seen it modeled for so long, and God had been faithful to stay close to his people. Joshua just said ok and rose to the occasion.

There comes a moment in every journey where God calls you from walking along the path and starts telling you to run. When it's time for the small steps to become great strides. That moment had come for Joshua, and it's coming for you.

Just like Joshua was challenged when the moment came, I'll challenge you—be strong and courageous. You've been walking long enough. Now it's time to run. But even after we hear the call, there's a war to fight before we move: the battle inside our minds.

THE INNER CRITIC

The moment we know it's time for the next step, intrusive thoughts often become the loudest. We become very aware of our shortcomings and realize that we are not qualified for the greatness we see in front of us. "I'm not enough." "I need more training, more time, more permission." Much like Moses, we can see all of the things that we feel disqualify us from the next step. Much like Moses, we can look at what is in our hands and say, "There's no way this is enough."

These thoughts are natural, but our response should be just as natural. The Bible tells us that we have power over our thoughts. When we recognize the thoughts that are coming against us, our purpose, and attacking our identity, we must eliminate them. We have to take them captive. They're a toxic, unwanted element in the garden of our mind. We can't write them off as poor self-esteem or even just a normal human response. Remember the warning we find in scripture:

> For we are not fighting against flesh-and-blood enemies, but against evil rulers and authorities of the unseen world, against mighty powers in this dark world, and against evil spirits in the heavenly places.
> Ephesians 6:12

Until we recognize and are aware of the way the enemy uses our own minds against us, we remain completely vulnerable to attack. When you don't realize an enemy is even there, you're not prepared to fight. You're literally just sitting down to a meal with him to talk about the day. Ignorance is *not* bliss, and there's no room for leaving our minds defenseless.

It's our responsibility to recognize the fight for our minds and take control of it. There is nothing that will take you out faster than the thoughts that no one else hears. The things that no one said. The situations that didn't happen. The things that happened in our minds. Our mind can convince us of just about anything, and we have to guard it. We have to realize the power of our mind, the fight over our thoughts. And that can't be a passive realization, but a war. Not in our own strength, thank goodness! We fight the unseen world with the unseen world. It's God who will do the fighting for us. But we do still have a role to play. And God has already given us all of the tools and weapons we need.

Let's take it back to the dirt, because that's where I see all of the principles of God so clearly. In a garden, when we start pulling out weeds that would choke out new growth of the plants you hope will flourish, there are a couple of things to keep in mind. I don't know how many weeds you've pulled in your day, but you can't just snap those suckers off. If you do it the lazy way, they're just going to keep growing back because you left the root in the ground. You have to dig down in there. You have to pull out the root to get rid of that weed. It

> You can get a garden looking good fairly easily, but to get it healthy takes the real work.

makes it much harder work! You can get a garden *looking* good fairly easily, but to get it *healthy* takes the real work.

Do. the. hard. work. WHY are these the thoughts that keep harassing me? WHY do I believe that about myself? WHAT underlying situation or thought pattern is shaping or limiting my thinking and beliefs?

Anything that convinces you that you are something other than what God speaks over you in Scripture needs to be rooted out. Dig out those roots by proclaiming scripture over yourself. Speak out loud the claims from scripture!

> We destroy arguments and every lofty opinion raised against the knowledge of God, and *take every thought captive* to obey Christ.
> 2 Corinthians 10:5 ESV

> For God has not given us a spirit of fear, but of power and of love and of a *sound mind*.
> 2 Timothy 1:7 NKJV

NOTE: We're going to the next step, but just because these are close together on the page doesn't make this a quick process. Give yourself some grace and time to discover, dig, heal and repair. Sometimes roots go deep and they're not destroyed in a moment. Ask for help. You may need a counselor for a season. It may be work that can be tackled by yourself and a close trusted friend. But it's a work worth doing, and it's a work that will require the Holy Spirit. This is not a fight of the flesh, so you'll never be able to win the fight in your own strength.

When we've dug in to get the roots out, we now have a little hole in our soil, and we need to fill it. Where we've removed the lie of the enemy, we have to fill with the truth of God's Word so there's not room for anything else.

> Think about the things of heaven, not the things of earth.
> Colossians 3:2

> And now, dear brothers and sisters, one final thing. Fix your thoughts on what is true, and honorable, and right, and pure, and lovely, and admirable. Think about things that are excellent and worthy of praise.
> Philippians 4:8

> But you belong to God, my dear children. You have already won a victory over those people, because the Spirit who lives in you is greater than the spirit who lives in the world.
> 1 John 4:4

As you begin this process (and don't let yourself forget that it's a process), it will seem to get worse than ever. (You thought I was going to say better, didn't you?) As you uproot all of the things that are damaging your ability to see yourself the way God sees you and created you, the enemy isn't going to be happy about it. You will find yourself in more situations that challenge your thinking than ever before. No enemy is known to wage war on a neutral threat, after all. Keep calling out to Jesus. Keep asking for his help as you fight the battle for your mind. And I can't stress this enough–do it with other people. We are made to be a body together, and we function best that way. Work through the process in community. You don't need to share your deepest thoughts and struggles with every person, but find people who build you up. People who understand the assignment. People who will call you higher, not lull you into giving up.

A true, godly community will be one that sees the good in you and calls it out. They will get excited over your wins, support you in the struggle, and be running alongside you because they're like-minded in seeking God's best. If this doesn't sound like your community, start praying. God has the right people out there. Pray that he would open your eyes to recognize the relationships that are like ankle weights while you run, and the relationships that will be the wind behind you. There's a huge difference, and you need the right people running with you.

THE WORLD NEEDS YOUR YES

We're in this together. The Bible says that we are a body. And every part of the body is needed to function as intended. It's easy to have a "grass is greener" approach to looking at the other parts, seeing the worth, beauty, or function of everything that is not yours. But the truth is, we're nothing without each other. Every single role holds importance when we're leaning on each other and walking in unity, like Jesus prayed we would.

> Yes, the body has many different parts, not just one part. If the foot says, "I am not a part of the body because I am not a hand," that does not make

it any less a part of the body. And if the ear says, "I am not part of the body because I am not an eye," would that make it any less a part of the body? If the whole body were an eye, how would you hear? Or if your whole body were an ear, how would you smell anything?

But our bodies have many parts, and God has put each part just where he wants it. How strange a body would be if it had only one part! Yes, there are many parts, but only one body. The eye can never say to the hand, "I don't need you." The head can't say to the feet, "I don't need you."

In fact, some parts of the body that <u>seem</u> weakest and least important are <u>actually</u> the most necessary. And the parts we regard as less honorable are those we clothe with the greatest care. So we carefully protect those parts that should not be seen, while the more honorable parts do not require this special care. So God has put the body together such that extra honor and care are given to those parts that have less dignity. This makes for harmony among the members, so that all the members care for each other. If one part suffers, all the parts suffer with it, and if one part is honored, all the parts are glad.

All of you together are Christ's body, and each of you is a part of it.

1 Corinthians 12:14-27

Even in the body, the parts that are the most important, the most unseen, are given the most attention. Not only are they necessary, but they also receive extra care. The leg might get a lot of compliments, be muscular and strong, but you could go a long time without bathing it. Then you have the armpit. I can't think of the last time someone complimented my armpit, but I put a lot more care into it. It's usually unseen, definitely not praised or photographed, but I'm going to take care to wash that sucker every day. I'm going to put deodorant on it and make sure it's good. The grass isn't greener. It's perspective. We all have different roles, they all look different on the outside, and they all need different levels of care. Don't despise being an armpit because it doesn't look like a leg.

We all have different capacities, and the reality of that has to be a part of realizing different people's roles in the body before you play the comparison game. The leg just isn't going to get the same care as an armpit, so it has to have a very high capacity, be able to do a lot of things for itself, and not need a lot of pats on the back and help along the way. The armpit is going to get the job done, but will need help and care to stay healthy so the rest of the body doesn't resent it when it starts stinking. Get it? This goes back to part one of the book, where we did a lot of personal inventory.

You have to come to a place where you understand who you are and how God made you, so you can see clearly how he has called you. He won't call you against your nature, so don't try to force yourself into someone else's narrative. (Note: he will always call you against your flesh nature, but not the nature that he has built inside of you!) The world needs YOUR yes. Not the yes you give while pretending to be something you wish you were. You are made the way you are with purpose. When we submit that to God and allow him to show us his intentions in it, we start to see the people, opportunities, and passions he's already placed in us and around us more clearly.

It is so easy to overlook the things that are special about yourself because they've always been a part of you. It's easy to point out something amazing about someone else because they walked into the room fresh. You've recently discovered something they've done. You were just introduced to their work. You weren't there for the process. You weren't there for the growth. From your side of the fence, you just don't know why the grass looks so darn green. You don't know how long they've been working, how many lessons they've learned, or if it's just green spray paint on that grass. The point is, you have something that only you have and only you can do. What if the thing you are discounting about yourself is someone else's answer to prayer? What if someone else's freedom is tied to your obedience?

The whole premise of our purpose being bigger than ourselves, something we can't attain by ourselves, is that it's not *for* ourselves. When you reach outside of yourself and what might bring you the biggest immediate reward, you'll start feeling more fulfilled. You'll begin to realize the big picture. There's just no part of this walk that is about us. Our worship is for God. Our serve is for people. Our purpose is for heaven. But man, when we embrace that truth and give *that* yes, you will start feeling like you *must* be God's favorite. You'll see the blessings he's promised. You'll experience the joy that comes with being a part of seeing

> What if someone else's freedom is tied to your obedience?

others experience life change in Jesus. Walking in purpose with Jesus is to fulfill the calling he placed on all of our lives. Every single person's purpose aligns with this:

> Therefore, go and make disciples of all the nations, baptizing them in the name of the Father and the Son and the Holy Spirit. Teach these new disciples to obey all the commands I have given you. And be sure of this: I am with you always, even to the end of the age.
> Matthew 28:19-20

So who are you to discount what the Lord has given you when he is the one who has called you, and this is our purpose? The way each of us completes this lifelong task will look different. But regardless of what part of the body you are, the rest of the body needs you. Your community needs you. Your family needs you. The world needs you. Your yes holds much more weight than what your 5-year plan might look like on paper. With all of the grace possible, realize that eternity hangs in the balance of your yes. Let your yes be a disruptor of plans. His plans are so much better. When you say yes, it's not just about you—it's about everyone who needs what you carry.

FROM INSECURITY TO IDENTITY

When you realize that your identity is rooted in Christ rather than who you are on your own, everything changes. You realize that the big, extraordinary callings aren't just for someone else, but they're yours as well. You realize that advocating for your child is as essential as pastoring people. Making decisions for your family is just as important as running a business. That living a generous life through success in the marketplace is just as important as being a missionary, when it's you're calling.

When we begin to realize that our identity is in Christ, the conversation shifts. You are able to move from "I'm not enough" to "He is enough in me." "What if I fail?" becomes "I follow a God who cannot fail." It's a shift of mindset that allows us to walk in authority and confidence with our head held high. Not because we've realized we're amazing, but because of the reality that it's not about us at all! When you allow the truth of who God is to permeate your thinking completely, you finally realize that you truly can't fail if you walk with him. Things may not look the way you want every step of the way. Things may take longer or be more challenging than we hope at times. But transformation is always happening in the trial.

As I have walked through trials and triumphs in life, I have come to realize that timing is everything. If I had been confronted with any situation that happened at any time before exactly when it happened, I would not have made it. But God is so gracious to grow us as we walk with him. When we say yes with our very little, he grows us. Then we keep walking and continue to grow. Before we know it, we have grown to be equipped for situations we were not equipped for before.

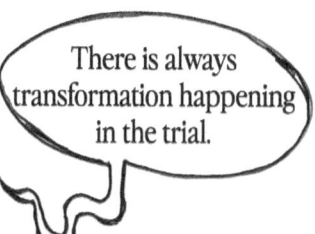

There is always transformation happening in the trial.

I think back to when we planted Cultivate Church. Before I got engaged to Brandon, there was a stipulation from the get-go. "Jen, we're going to plant a church at some point. Are you in for that?" "Sure thing." Oh, Jen. What a naive answer. Maybe sometimes ignorance may actually be bliss. Had I known what that meant at the time, I would have been overwhelmed and may or may not have been on board. But God, in his extreme faithfulness and understanding of my limited mind, allowed me to give an excited and ignorant YES!

I'd say I had very little to offer when we started, but in truth, I couldn't even find my seed. It may have fallen out of my pocket or something. Because really, I didn't feel like it was little, it felt like nothing. But the ingredients to a miracle are sometimes a yes, some excitement, and grit that refuses to quit. He started revealing things to me that would be helpful. My design skills were growing—helpful. I could sing—helpful. I had an unrelenting attention to detail—helpful...and hurtful. But he has grown me! I found my seeds, and God grew them along the way. And just like a Giant Redwood doesn't pop up overnight, steady growth amounts to amazing things.

God is faithful to complete the work HE has started in us. He's not going to leave us in our little offering. But he's only going to grow it when we're giving it back to him and walking faithfully alongside him. Say yes with your little. Even when it feels like the dust of where the seed used to be.

The enemy would have you keep your focus on yourself because that's where we fail. Any time things get hard, it's the enemy's opportunity to say, "I told you so." But we have to have the wherewithal to say, "No, you're not getting a foothold here. I'm standing with God at my side, and in my weakness, he is going to show up and show out. Sit back and watch."

Stay alert! Watch out for your great enemy, the
devil. He prowls around like a roaring lion,
looking for someone to devour.
1 Peter 5:8

Other translations start out by saying, 'Stay alert!' They both say
the same thing, but I love the wording of 'be sober-minded.' 'Stay
alert' can seem hyper to me, but 'sober-minded' gives me the
imagery of a clear head. Someone who isn't easily freaked out by
what the enemy is doing, but ready and prepared to respond.
Someone who realizes their calling comes from the Lord and is
ready to guard it against even the most minor work of the enemy.
It's not the huge mistakes the enemy is after. It's the slow, steady
drift (a small compromise here, a little apathy there) that will land
you miles from where you were meant to be.

The work we are doing is not our own, so we can't look to
ourselves as the source. We have to take hold of the truth that our
worth was settled on the cross. We will never grow into being
worthy. We'll never earn the status of righteous. We are made
righteous and worthy only because of Jesus. That's where our
identity is found, and that's the rock we stand on. We just have to
live like it's true, with no second-guessing the work he's done.

For we are God's masterpiece. He has created us
anew in Christ Jesus, so we can do the good things
he planned for us long ago.
Ephesians 2:10

ACT LIKE YOU MATTER

"I wish I could show you, when you are lonely or in darkness, the astonishing light of your own being." —Hafiz of Shiraz

Here's the thing. We've gone over the information. I've given you the scriptures. You have to do the work of realizing your value. And it's constant work. An important thing to remember is that it's work we are all doing constantly. The person beside you who appears to have it all together has the same internal conversations over insecurities. They may just be doing a better job fighting that day. Hear me when I say—you are not the only one who wonders if they matter. So stand up and do the thing even if you're shaking. The confidence will build as you keep fighting the fight in your mind and begin to see the truth from God's Word as it plays out in real life. You'll only see it if you start to move.

Where Moses hesitated, Joshua moved. What if you did too?

What if you woke up tomorrow and lived your day like you knew you mattered? Like you realized that every choice you made affected the world around you and held weight in others' lives. What if you woke up and reminded yourself that "We are God's masterpiece. He has created us anew in Christ Jesus, so we can do the good things he planned for us long ago." (Ephesians 2:20) Oh wait, if that's true, then every interaction I have today has a purpose. The job I'm in has a purpose today. The neighborhood I live in has people who might need me. The gym I go to is full of people whom I could impact. The homeschool group we're a part of has families that need community.

The older I get, the fewer coincidences I believe happen. I can see more purpose now in every detail than I ever could years ago. I can see the hand of God in every detail of the way a day, a process, or a plan comes together. And I pray that your eyes would open in the same way. To see the little things that he drops into your day to remind you that he sees you. Yes, that was there on purpose so you would be reminded of a prayer you prayed, or a dream you had. Notice the song in the background. Notice the sunset after a rough day. Notice the polite driver in a world of rude ones. Notice the little things that speak volumes, and realize that you do matter. You do hold weight. And all of your yeses mean something.

BREAK THE SMALLNESS

This chapter requires some action. I don't want you to move on before confronting all of the thoughts and feelings you had while reading. And if you didn't have any thoughts or feelings, then go ahead and look up a good Christian counselor close to you, because there might be more work to do than a journal can handle. I kid. (Not really. You should probably talk to someone.) This is something we all deal with on some level. Some of us have gotten better at fighting it over the years, and it looks different than when we started, but insecurities and the space we take up in the world is something that we all think about.

Play along with me. Spend some time thinking about this before you move on, because if this is left as a missing link, you'll keep hitting a wall.

- Write down three thoughts that are keeping you playing small.

Be honest. This isn't for anyone else. You can throw it away later if you need to, but we can't fight what we won't acknowledge.

- Write down a truth of God that combats each of them.

Google it. You don't have the know the Bible by heart. Discover what his Word says!

- Choose one action to take this week that scares you a little but aligns with your purpose.

Don't overthink this. You don't have to quit your job or move to another state. Send a text to build a friendship with someone you've been wanting to get to know better. Sign up to serve at your church. Go to a Bible study or small group so you can start building community. Write the article. Ask the question. What is it for you?

Then pray, pray, pray that God would align your sight and your thinking with his. We can be so blind to our own reality. We're with us every day, after all! It can be hard to see the amazing things, the potential we have, and how all of the dots connect in an incredible way that is yours and yours alone. Pray that God would open your eyes to see what he sees.

> You were never meant to blend in. You were made to break ground.

This isn't a one-and-done, friend. You're going to have to keep praying this prayer and keep asking the questions. But you can do it. And it will be worth it. You were never meant to blend in.

You were made to break ground. Your yes shakes heaven and shifts earth. Act like you matter. Because you do.

08
THE COST OF YOUR CALLING—
Why Greatness Requires More Than Good Intentions

Let's be real, everybody loves the idea of God's promises. We just don't want the bill that comes with it. Somewhere along the way, we began to think that we could step into greatness with good intentions alone. That if we wanted it bad enough, it would just happen. But real greatness (the kind that lasts) comes with a price tag. Not because God is holding out on us, but because he's growing something in us. It's the daily choices no one sees. The sacrifices no one applauds. The steady faith when quitting would be easier. If you want to live the life God promised you, you're going to have to pay the price. I can tell you, it's worth every single thing you lay down.

If we can find an example in the Bible of someone practicing what they preach, it's Paul. Beaten, imprisoned, stoned, shipwrecked, insulted, misunderstood, but he continued to walk in his calling. He says in 2 Corinthians 4:13, "We continue to preach because we have the same kind of faith the psalmist had when he said, 'I believe in God, so I spoke.'" God said it, so Paul determined he would continue moving forward. Paul doesn't just endure hardship; he reframes it. His letters remind us that suffering isn't a detour from our purpose; it's part of the path. In Romans 5, he shows us how endurance becomes the gateway to strength and hope…

> We can rejoice, too, when we run into problems
> and trials, for we know that they help us develop
> endurance. And endurance develops strength of
> character, and character strengthens our confident
> hope of salvation.
> Romans 5:3-4

Endurance isn't gifted. It's earned. Think about a runner. Whether you run or not, you are likely able to realize that no one wakes up one day and, having never run before, decides to run a marathon. Endurance is something that has to be built in our physical body. A runner builds endurance by running more and more as they train. Learning how to pace themselves. Learning what their body needs to go a long distance without failing. They learn how to listen to their body and take care of it as they build to the goal distance they want to run.

You don't have to be a runner to understand the reality of it. You can be someone that had to run after a child, sprint to catch a friend, or engage in a little Thanksgiving Day soccer in the backyard. You 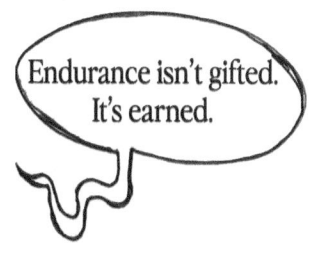 don't go into a high-exertion activity unprepared and feel excited and full of life afterward. You feel sweaty and out of breath!

Just as our physical endurance is built through daily physical activity, spiritual endurance is developed through daily obedience. Even when it's hard. Even when we have to do it alone. Even when it feels slow. However, when we make tough decisions, we become stronger and our character is built. Every decision to listen to what the Holy Spirit is speaking to us puts a little more distance on our run. Every time we make a decision to obey, it expands our lungs just a little more. Every time we walk towards our calling rather than towards what is comfortable, our O2 levels climb just a little more. Endurance is earned through daily paying the price.

I started praying years ago that no ministry I'm a part of and no calling on my life would ever outgrow my character. God has answered that prayer. Do I feel like some things have taken longer than expected to grow like I want? Of course. But you know what I haven't done along the way? Crashed and burned. I haven't gone through seasons of burnout that made me question what I was doing. Have I gone through hard times? Exhausting seasons? Of course. But in working through the hard things, I've been able to build longevity. A sprint is awesome, but that's not what greatness is. True greatness will go the distance. It realizes that this calling is bigger than ourselves and what it might look like for our own lives.

It wonders what impact it will have on others. And no one is looking for a moment. They're looking for a legacy. But that kind of greatness requires a process that not everyone is willing to wait for and work through.

SOMETHING FOR NOTHING IS A LIE

We live in a culture that is looking for something for nothing. To put in work or have to wait is unacceptable. We don't like waiting in lines. We have all of the answers we could ever want at our fingertips. We can have our groceries delivered in time to make dinner with them. There are reading clubs that exist only of 10-15 minute summaries of books so you can consume information without actually have to read. Fast food, overnight shipping, instant downloads. I want my stuff now, I want my reward now, I want my way now. If it isn't quick, we question if it's even worth it.

Somewhere along the line, that mindset slipped into our faith, too. We want the rewards of obedience without the grind of daily obedience. We want the promises without the process. But that's not how greatness is built in the Kingdom of God. It's not flashy. It's not instant. It's steady, unseen faithfulness. Few and far between are the people who are willing to stick out the hard stuff for a reward that is greater than what is available in an instant.

While looking for the big, instant payoff, we're overlooking the simplest acts of obedience. While we long for the quick, here we sit. Walking through one thing that just can't be fast. We sit in something that Nietzsche would call a "long obedience in the same direction." Building strength and character and practicing perseverance, even when the results aren't immediate. It's the absolute opposite of our fast-paced society. So let me ask you–are you building for a moment or for a legacy? Are your daily choices laying bricks for eternity, or are you chasing the instant rewards of a world that doesn't last?

Is reading the Bible every single day life-changing in any given moment? Maybe not every time. Does it culminate in a rich, deep relationship with the Lord? Oh, absolutely yes. Does prayer sometimes feel like talking to a brick wall? Sure. Is the habit of taking all of your thanks, needs, hopes, and desires before God building relationship even when you can't feel it? You bet it is.

We want the miraculous, but we overlook the mundane. We ask God for mountain-moving faith, but roll our eyes at the daily disciplines He has already placed in our hands. But what if the very thing we're calling "nothing" is what God is using to build everything?

Some of the most transformational work God does in your life happens in moments that may seem unimpressive. It looks like waking up a little earlier to pray when you'd rather be sleeping. Opening your Bible when no one is looking. Speaking truth when silence would be easier. Saying no to an opportunity that would elevate you in people's eyes but compromise what God told you in private. Forgiving someone who never apologized, because obedience matters more than justice. Tithing faithfully when money is tight and no one's clapping for your generosity.

> What God wants to build through you can't stand on shortcuts.

These are the bricks. The unseen, ordinary, un-glamorous steps that lay the foundation for true greatness in the purpose God has laid out for you. You can easily underestimate the work that is being done, but it's building something eternal. These quiet choices shape your character. What God wants to build through you can't stand on shortcuts. It's a long obedience in the same direction.

Are you willing to do the lackluster daily walking to make your way to the compounding results? We're called not to walk on our own, but to walk closely with the Lord. To commit to a long obedience in the same direction.

SCRIPTURE ISN'T OPTIONAL—IT'S SURVIVAL

> Remain in me, and I will remain in you. For a branch cannot produce fruit if it is severed from the vine, and you cannot be fruitful unless you remain in me. Yes, I am the vine; you are the branches. Those who remain in me, and I in them, will produce much fruit. For apart from me you can do nothing.
> John 15:4-5

And how do we remain in him? Through getting to know him and walking the way he's instructed us to walk. How do we get to know him? Read the Bible to discover HIM rather than ourselves. Look for his character and the things that are important to him. It shifted my entire world to realize that the Bible wasn't about me! But when you read to see how God treated people and why he responded in different ways, you can truly fall in love with the Living God and his Word.

> But they delight in the law of the Lord, meditating on it day and night. They are like trees planted along the riverbank, bearing fruit each season. Their leaves never wither, and they prosper in all they do.
> Psalms 1:2-3

Why don't these trees wither? They are planted by the source. Constantly drawing water from the river. When we're making the commitment to stay in his Word consistently, the cost honestly starts feeling like less and less of a burden because our spirits begin to thrive!

There are many "truths" being thrown at us constantly in culture that are completely different from what we find in the Word of God. If we don't KNOW the Word of God, they'll be very easily mistaken for truth. So many things are very spiritual and sound very close to what we believe, but they're missing the life-changing power of Jesus. We can easily rationalize plenty of things in culture if we don't know what God actually says about them.

Jesus was in conversation with a religious leader who was asking questions about how to interpret a particular scripture. "Jesus replied, 'Your mistake is that you don't know the Scriptures, and you don't know the power of God.'" (Mark 12:24) This person was not someone new to the Bible, but a Bible teacher. He "knew" the Scripture. You can be familiar with the contents without understanding the power. You can read without being changed. You can know without understanding.

Are you reading to know and understand? Are you reading to follow rules or fall in love? When was the last time the Word of God actually *stopped you in your tracks*? Do you read just to get through it, or to let it dwell in you and change you?

> Commit yourselves wholeheartedly to these words
> of mine. Tie them to your hands and wear them on
> your forehead as reminders. Teach them to your
> children. Talk about them when you are at home
> and when you are on the road, when you are going
> to bed and when you are getting up. Write them on
> the doorposts of your house and on your gates, so
> that as long as the sky remains above the earth,
> you and your children may flourish in the land the
> Lord swore to give your ancestors.
> Deuteronomy 11:18-21

Knowing the Lord and knowing his Word is what keeps us close to him. That's how we remain in him. It's not by good intentions, being a good person, or going to church. It's by clinging to his Word. He says to be careful to obey and hold tightly to the Lord. (Deuteronomy 11:22) There's a reason for that. It's because the enemy knows what we're called to do and if there's room for distraction or confusion, he'll insert it. Hold tightly to the Lord and be careful to obey.

Go after the things that are keeping you from the fullness of God. This isn't an area where it's ok to sit idly by and hope for the best. There's a whole section of scripture dedicated to making sure we understand we have armor available to us and we need to get up and put it on every day. (Refresh yourself in Ephesians 6:10-18.) In case you need reminding, there is only one weapon and that's the Sword of the Spirit. The Word of God. We fight by knowing what the Word says and understanding the power it holds. Do something with what the Word of God tells us. There's no sense in knowing Scripture if we're not going to put it into practice. This is how we protect what's ours. Are you willing to fight for it?

THE CALL TO GREATNESS

Greatness will cost you something. While sometimes the cost will be significant or require a lot of thought and sacrifice, often it is small, ordinary steps that we'd rather just push aside as unimportant. Inconsequential. But if God has asked it of us, how inconsequential could it possibly be? In following the Lord, I have yet to find something that he has done just for kicks. Everything in the Bible is intentionally connected because it serves a purpose. Not one detail happens by chance. So why would we think our lives would be any different? He has laid out a clear path for how to get close to him. He has offered it up for us to read in black and white, and still we ask why he feels so far away. Why am I not making headway in this area of my life? Well, have you followed the instructions?

You saw me before I was born.
Every day of my life was recorded in your book.

Every moment was laid out
  before a single day had passed.
Psalm 139:16

Before you were born, God set your journey with intention. There is a purpose. There is a goal. There is greatness. Don't forget–we can't get held up on words like "greatness" and "calling" when it comes to our faith, like they're reserved for people in full-time ministry. If you haven't heard it before, your life is your ministry. Are you a stay-at-home mom? Ministry. Are you a consultant? Ministry. Are you an investor? Ministry. Educator? Ministry. Whatever position you hold in life holds purpose and significance. When you choose to see it that way, you realize the way God has his hand on your every step. To realize that you're raising children who need your hand and guidance so they can, in turn, walk in their purpose, allows you to see the intentionality in your parenting. To look around your workplace and see all of the people that you have influence over will change your interactions with people. To be raking in the big bucks and realize that your heart of generosity is God-breathed brings meaning to something that could feel detached from a work of God.

If every moment is already seen by God, then every obedient step, big or small, echoes in eternity. What we hold in our hands is holy, and the intention we put into every day should reflect that we understand that. God hasn't given any of us something worthless. But when we compare what's in our hands to someone else's, we can treat what he sees as holy as something common or flippant.

We think greatness is in the spotlight moments. But David understood that true greatness is often revealed in what we're willing to give up behind closed doors. When we view what God has given us as something holy to be stewarded well, we can more easily see the cost attached. David understood there was a cost. When tempted with the "easy way out" of this cost, King David refused and insisted on paying the cost. David said, "I will not offer burnt offerings to the Lord my God that cost me nothing." (2 Samuel 24:24) Even the king, a man who had achieved cultural greatness, knew that meant nothing in the Kingdom of God. That if his worship didn't come from his energy and his resources, it meant nothing.

Elijah understood the same thing. In 1 Kings 17, Elijah prayed that there would be no rain for the next few years until he gave the word. So be it. There was no rain. Three years into the drought, Elijah came to call for a showdown between the prophets of Baal and the Living God. The people were wavering between Baal and the Lord, and Elijah had had enough. You're going to choose today.

The prophets of Baal were going to sacrifice a bull on their altar, and Elijah was going to sacrifice a bull on the altar of the Lord. Neither one was going to set it on fire, but they were going to *pray* that it would catch fire so they could see which god was the true one. The prophets of Baal sacrificed a bull on their altar and prayed and hollered and cut themselves and acted a fool all day long and that altar never caught fire.

Then it was Elijah's turn.

Now, obviously, God *wants* to show the people that he is the true God—the one and only. I feel like Elijah could have walked into this situation with some pretty solid confidence. But instead of walking in assumptions, Elijah prepared an offering. He got the bull ready on the altar, then had the people dump water all over the altar, the sacrifice, and even filled a trench around the altar. 12 large jars of water were poured out.

Now, this is a setup for a cool party trick. When God sends fire and this wet altar is engulfed in flames, it's going to be the coolest thing ever! But water was scarce. Like, really scarce. Elijah offered something precious. An offering that meant something. He covered this sacrifice with a costly offering.

God, indeed, sent fire from heaven and engulfed the altar in flames and drank up every drop of water. Elijah's heart and prayer were for the people to come back to the Lord. He was there out of obedience, he poured out a costly offering, and "when the people saw it, they fell face down on the ground and cried out, 'The Lord–he is God! Yes, the Lord is God!'" (1 Kings 18:39) Elijah's yes resulted in greatness.

COUNT THE COST

Each one of us will pay a cost to follow Jesus and walk in greatness. That won't look the same for all of us.

> As Jesus was starting out on his way to Jerusalem, a man came running up to him, knelt down, and asked, "Good Teacher, what must I do to inherit eternal life?" "Why do you call me good?" Jesus asked. "Only God is truly good. But to answer your question, you know the commandments:

'You must not murder. You must not commit adultery. You must not steal. You must not testify falsely. You must not cheat anyone. Honor your father and mother.'" "Teacher," the man replied, "I've obeyed all these commandments since I was young." Looking at the man, Jesus felt genuine love for him. "There is still one thing you haven't done," he told him. "Go and sell all your possessions and give the money to the poor, and you will have treasure in heaven. Then come, follow me." At this the man's face fell, and he went away sad, for he had many possessions.

Mark 10:17-22

This guy loved Jesus! He followed all of the commandments. Since he was young, he says. That means this had been a lifelong journey so far for him, and he was so excited to talk to Jesus and wanted the next steps. But in the end went away sad because he just wasn't willing to pay the cost. To lay down the thing that was holding more of his heart than Jesus.

Following Jesus will cost each of us something. And often, it's the very thing that makes us hesitate. For this rich man, it was his wealth. For some, it's popularity. For some, it's status. Comfort. Many things might stand in the way, and the reasons are likely to differ greatly between us. What's the thing in your hands that's too expensive to lay down, but more expensive to keep?

I have been in moments when it felt hard to walk out decisions I had made because they didn't make sense to the people around me. My husband and I decided from the beginning to be intentional with our marriage. We know that long-lasting relationships don't happen by accident, so we made up our minds to never take it for granted, but to make decisions that would protect it before there was anything to worry about. That meant being firm on things like neither of us riding in the car alone with the opposite sex. That doesn't sound like that big of a deal, right? The thing is, when you are in a work environment where you're supposed to ride across town with a male co-worker and you say no, well, that doesn't always go over very well.

I remember feeling a particular tension after I stood my ground, but didn't realize until much later that I almost lost my job because of it! The people around me didn't understand, or care, why I had made that decision and why it was an important one to stand by. But for us, it was firm. I stood by it and God showed me favor with my boss, and I kept my job. Because it was a predetermined conviction that I would be loyal to, regardless of job security, my answer would have been the same. If Daniel could pray in the face of death, it didn't seem like too big of a sacrifice to risk my job to protect my marriage.

The more you make the small decisions, the more faith you have for the next one. Then the more faith you have for the bigger one that comes along. Even when you do it scared, it counts! It's remembering that it's not our strength that's carrying us that takes the load off.

THE BLESSING ON THE OTHER SIDE OF OBEDIENCE

There is a lot of promise and potential tied up in trusting the Lord and just taking the steps, one after the other. Extraordinary purpose requires radical obedience, but often, our Western-thinking brains are programmed to need proof before belief. We tend to be people who want certainty, clarity, and full understanding before we move. Before we trust. But God doesn't promise to provide those answers every time.

Let's look at another story from Elijah's life. This happens before the fire showdown we just read about.

> Then the Lord said to Elijah, "Go and live in the village of Zarephath, near the city of Sidon. I have instructed a widow there to feed you." *(Let that sit in your mind for a moment. The Lord had already picked her out and spoken to her.)*
>
> So he went to Zarephath. As he arrived at the gates of the village, he saw a widow gathering sticks, and he asked her, "Would you please bring me a little water in a cup?" As she was going to get it, he called to her, "Bring me a bite of bread, too."
>
> But she said, "I swear by the Lord your God that I don't have a single piece of bread in the house. And I have only a handful of flour left in the jar and a little cooking oil in the bottom of the jug. I was just gathering a few sticks to cook this last meal, and then my son and I will die."
>
> But Elijah said to her, "Don't be afraid! Go ahead and do just what you've said, but make a little bread for me first. Then use what's left to prepare a meal for yourself and your son. For this

> is what the Lord, the God of Israel, says: There
> will always be flour and olive oil left in your
> containers until the time when the Lord sends rain
> and the crops grow again!"
>
> 1 Kings 17:8-14 (commentary added by me)

Can you imagine 'ol boy coming in and asking for your last meal? You're telling him you guys are about to curl up and die, and he doesn't even address it. Elijah doesn't coddle their death statement because he knew she was speaking out of fear. Fear paralyzes you. But we're not supposed to operate under a spirit of fear, but of power, love, and a sound mind. We have to make what we DO know of God bigger than what we DON'T know of the future.

> So she did as Elijah said, *(even though it didn't
> add up)* and she and Elijah and her family
> continued to eat for many days. There was always
> enough flour and olive oil left in the containers,
> just as the Lord had promised through Elijah.
>
> 1 Kings 17:15 (2 cents added by me)

Jehovah Jireh. The Lord will provide. We can also see him as El Roi here. The God who sees me. God had already chosen her, seen her need, and decided to provide for her *following* her obedience.

The Lord had spoken to her and told her to do what Elijah said. We don't know how much time passed between that and Elijah showing up, but she had time to think about the weight of it, then came the opportunity to obey or not. To say yes in the face of what you see as a death sentence. You can believe she counted the cost. And she didn't pay it flippantly.

The next big step, the sacrifice, the unknown, doesn't become more comfortable the more you believe. The stronger you get. You do it afraid. But you do it anointed. We don't become fearless, we just become more faith-full. We see it over and over again – obedience opens the door to blessings in your life.

THOSE CUTE, HORRIBLE LITTLE FOXES

The daily obedience that protects your purpose takes diligence. The Enemy is crafty but not very creative. He's always going to be up to the same tricks, and those tricks can be easy to overlook because it's usually going to be a small little bugger. If he comes at you with something huge, you'll probably sit up and recognize it in a second. You'll probably call someone to pray with you or help you course correct. It's not that he will never attack in that way, but for the day-to-day, he's smarter than that. He knows that the little things can go unnoticed for a long time. Sometimes they remain unnoticed until the fall-out is devastating.

Scripture warns us to "Catch all the foxes, those little foxes, before they ruin the vineyard of love, for the grapevines are blossoming!" (Song of Songs 2:15)

Little foxes are a big deal in a vineyard because to eat the fruit from the vine that they are too small to reach, they chew at the bottom of the vine so it falls and they can get the fruit. Instead of just climbing up and eating the fruit, they destroy the years of cultivating that went into growing the vine.

These little foxes in our lives aren't trying to make your small group fail or a friendship go bad. They're not trying to discourage or frustrate you; they're after your roots. They're trying to level you. They're out to destroy your foundation. All of your growth and maturity. All you've worked through and fought for up to this point.

Little foxes look different in all of our lives, but there are a lot of consistent culprits. Compromise, laziness, people-pleasing, inconsistency. The neglect in daily prayer, glitches in our integrity, and lack of private disciplines. They may seem like minor missteps in the moment, but they're eroding the very roots of greatness. It's like a beautiful vineyard that's slowly collapsing. Not from one big storm, but from tiny foxes day after day chewing at the roots. The small, consistent acts of obedience are the ones that build a firm foundation. They're the decisions that protect your roots.

There is a cost to greatness because greatness doesn't happen on its own. It happens when we walk hand in hand with the Lord. Are we walking close enough to him to be able to catch the small compromises before they destroy the vineyard? What's nibbling at your roots while you're busy polishing your branches or admiring your fruit?

What's nibbling at your roots while you're busy polishing your branches or admiring your fruit?

CHOOSE TO PAY THE PRICE

To walk in the greatness that God has called us to will require a cost. It will demand decisions of us that don't always make sense to the culture around us. It involves protecting yourself, your spirit, your marriage, your family, your walk with the Lord, your convictions, and your dreams with a fierce resolve and an impenetrable barrier.

Little foxes can sneak into the smallest crack. But staying in the Word, spending time with the Lord, and keeping your eyes fixed on him is like sealing those cracks with concrete. Keeping every potential crack patched up and strong.

Take some time to look closely at your life. Look at your weaknesses. Look at where the little foxes might be able to wear you down, and pay the price to keep them out. Greatness in the sense we're talking about won't look like what the world would consider greatness. But it will be richer. It will have a lasting impact. It will be full.

What are your little foxes?

What is the cost you need to pay?

Choose to embrace the cost, knowing the greatness of walking with Jesus far outweighs anything you lay down. The promise stands, but the price still holds. Are you willing to pay the price for the greatness God has placed in your hands?

09
WHEN THE DUST SETTLES

"You can't add days to your life, but you can add life to your days." –Unknown

> How do you know what your life will be like
> tomorrow? Your life is like the morning fog—it's
> here a little while, then it's gone.
> James 4:14

You are someone's ancestor. That really should shift the way we live. It doesn't take much thought or contemplation to realize that life is fleeting. The older we get, the faster the weeks fly by. We have the choice to waste our days in the moment, or spend them on what will last. Even better, *invest* them in what will come after us. The people we look up to most have done something that has left a lasting impact. A parent who believed in their child despite the odds. A leader that empowered rather than hogging the glory. A business owner who coached rather than gate-kept. When we're willing to invest in the ones that will replace us one day, we take a mortal life and make it last. It's easy to think of what we leave behind in material terms: wealth, a business, a home. But legacy isn't a possession to pass down—it's a purpose to steward. A spiritual inheritance to multiply. All of the things that can be tracked from a human perspective pale in comparison to the spiritual legacy we can leave.

> I once thought these things were valuable, but now I consider them worthless because of what Christ has done. Yes, everything else is worthless when compared with the infinite value of knowing Christ Jesus my Lord. For his sake I have discarded everything else, counting it all as garbage, so that I could gain Christ.
> Philippians 3:7-8

As this scripture points out, *things* are worthless compared to what Christ has done. Our ultimate legacy lies not in the *things* we leave behind but in how we steward the time we were given. Every yes we say to God echoes beyond our lifetime, rippling through generations as a testimony of trust and obedience. The qualities that make up our lives (relationships, careers, hobbies, etc) are things the Lord has entrusted us to steward well while we are here. Are you treating what he's given you as a gift, or are you comparing it to someone else? Are you holding what he's given you like it's holy, or are you tucking it away until it looks more impressive?

> Legacy isn't a possession to pass down—it's a purpose to steward.

We are called to live a life that leaves an impact, but you won't be handed the full picture at once. I will never forget driving with my dad to my Grandaddy's funeral. I have so much respect for him, and it is a great loss to know a world without him. I said, "There just aren't men like him anymore." My dad just said, "Well, you know he wasn't always that man. He grew into the man you know." And my vision shifted in an instant. I wasn't the woman I used to be. I won't be the woman I am now years into the future. We are all building our legacy every day as we grow into the person God has called us to be. This should come as no surprise to you by now, but it reminds me of growing a plant.

If you've ever seen a packet of seeds, it usually has a picture of the full-grown plant on the front. The seed inside bears no resemblance to where that plant is headed when it's placed into the soil. It doesn't look like the picture when it's watered and tended to before the sprout ever emerges from the soil. It doesn't look like the picture as the fragile little shoot starts to grow.

Just enough light. Plenty of water. Don't ignore it or it will break, burn, or shrivel. Eventually, that shoot gets a little more hearty. Ok, we're not as nervous about it sustaining life now. Whew. But we've still got a long way to go. A lot of growth, and a lot of change. Depending on the seed you've planted, you may not be far from seeing a resemblance to the picture on the seed packet. You may have fruit soon. You may have branches on the way. Or maybe the bud of a flower is forming. But it doesn't happen all at once, and you just can't rush it.

When God places something in your hand for you to steward, he's not just handing you a little seed. He already sees what that seed is going to grow into. He's saying, "Stick with me. We've got places to go. We have a lot of growth to walk through. Can you wait well? Can you do the work when you can't see the growth happening?"

That's the hard part. The waiting. The trusting. So many stick that seed right into their pocket because it doesn't look impressive. Something that small takes time. Sometimes it takes a lot of time. And if you think about a plant, a lot of the growth happens under the soil first. When the seed is underground, a lot is happening to it that we can't see. The seed is breaking open. The tiny little growth begins to emerge from the seed. And these are the hard parts to wait through because it can feel like all of your praying, all of your investing into your purpose, all of the obedience is going unnoticed. Unfortunately, many people give up underground. But God is asking us to wait well. Do the work to live on mission with him because the growth is happening. And at just the right time, you'll see the results.

This is where so many give up

Right before you see results.

Jesus also said, "The Kingdom of God is like a farmer who scatters seed on the ground. Night and day, while he's asleep or awake, the seed sprouts and grows, but he does not understand how it happens. The earth produces the crops on its own. First, a leaf blade pushes through, then the heads of wheat are formed, and finally the grain ripens."
Mark 4:26-28

Did you catch that? The growth wasn't in the farmer's control. He planted the seed and trusted the process. God has given you a seed. You don't have the ability or the power to rush it, to make it grow faster, or to change it from an apple tree to a lemon tree. All you can do is be a good steward of your seed by planting it and taking care of it. Then trust God to do the work. You'll grow into something you didn't think was possible when you let God do the work. But you've got to get that seed out of your pocket, say yes, and plant the seed.

As we set our sights on living with meaning rather than living for fleeting moments, we make an impact on the people who are watching us grow. Sometimes it's your child, and you know you need to be a good example as a parent. But a lot of times, people are watching that you don't even realize. I tell our worship team all of the time that I love how everyone on the team is so different because we will all be able to resonate with a different person we're leading. You are someone's person. Someone in your sphere of influence sees the growth. They see you control your anger where you didn't before. They have noticed you being more generous. They have followed in your example of shutting down gossip. You are someone's person.

I worked in a department store when I started following Jesus, and there was a woman who worked across the department from me. I remember it like it happened yesterday. We were in a conversation with a mutual friend, and she said, "Well, God can just use anybody, can't he?" I wasn't sure how to take that, but I decided to take it as a compliment! Through a loose connection from across a department store, someone was watching, and Jesus was showing. You are someone's person, and God is doing the work even when it feels slow.

As we recognize that truth, let's put some intention to it.

A LEGACY THAT OUTLASTS YOU

> But those who wish to boast should boast in this
> alone: that they truly know me and understand that
> I am the Lord.
> Jeremiah 9:24

As Christ-followers, we know that our life on earth isn't meant to be fleeting, but something that changes the people around us. That's the calling we all have in common. To go and make disciples, then teach those disciples to follow Jesus. (Matthew 28:19-20) Regardless of how it plays out in each of our lives—the career path, the relationships, the ways we serve others—the common thread is that we are to find a way for our journey to point people to Jesus.

When it comes to leaving a legacy, something that will live beyond our time on earth, we have to remember that it isn't something that magically appears when we're gone. Our legacy is being built every day. Often in much smaller ways than we realize. The way we treat people. The time we spend with the Lord that the younger ones get to witness. The intentionality with our words and wealth. These are things that make an impact on people little by little as you live with purpose consistently. Moses charges the people of Israel with this when he says, "You must commit yourselves wholeheartedly to these commands that I am giving you today. Repeat them again and again to your children. Talk about them when you are at home and when you are on the road, when you are going to bed and when you are getting up. Tie them to your hands and wear them on your forehead as reminders. Write them on the doorposts of your house and on your gates." (Deuteronomy 6:6-9)

We are to make it a part of who we are. Ingrained into our everyday lives, so there is no question. THIS is why I live. THIS is where I find my motivation, my vision, and my reason. EVEN when you can't see the growth that's happening. It's a life mission. Not a project to try out for a bit. Living with meaning in the way we're called takes a full commit. Jesus changed my life, now I'll give it back to him. Legacy isn't accidental. It's built by choice. Sustained by faith. Cemented by consistency.

> So here's what I want you to do, God helping you:
> Take your everyday, ordinary life—your sleeping,
> eating, going-to-work, and walking-around life—
> and place it before God as an offering. Embracing

what God does for you is the best thing you can do for him. Don't become so well-adjusted to your culture that you fit into it without even thinking. Instead, fix your attention on God. You'll be changed from the inside out. Readily recognize what he wants from you, and quickly respond to it. Unlike the culture around you, always dragging you down to its level of immaturity, God brings the best out of you, develops well-formed maturity in you.
Romans 12:2 MSG

This is our charge:

> We will not hide these truths from our children;
>   we will tell the next generation
> about the glorious deeds of the Lord,
>   about his power and his mighty wonders.
>
> For he issued his laws to Jacob;
>   he gave his instructions to Israel.
> He commanded our ancestors
>   to teach them to their children,
>
> so the next generation might know them—
>   even the children not yet born—
>   and they in turn will teach their own children.

> So each generation should set its hope anew on
> God, not forgetting his glorious miracles
>   and obeying his commands.
> Psalm 78:4-7

That's a lot of scripture, but that's our mission. It's bigger than today, and it's bigger than ourselves. It takes our constant attention and intention.

When we live with purpose, there is a weight to the steps we take. We understand that we want to stand tall so that the next generation can stand on our shoulders and see farther. We realize that our yes has very little to do with our personal gain in the moment and a whole lot to do with the people around us and the ones to come after.

THE MOSES MODEL

We've talked about Moses a lot throughout this book. Such an amazing leader, prophet, and friend of God. When he finally got to the end of his life, we see a beautiful picture of a leader moving on. Deuteronomy 34 tells us that Moses was still as strong as ever, and his eyesight was clear. The people mourned for him for 30 days, and if you read through the Old Testament, you will feel that weight when you get to this part of the story. This was a man who carried influence, learned a lot of lessons, empowered leaders, and interceded for people. When it made sense to give up or walk away, he pleaded with God on their behalf. He loved them and gave his life to lead them because God had called him.

Moses was an amazing father of the faith. And if we left it at that, he would still be a great man and leader. But it doesn't end there. When Moses knew it was his time to pass, he was intentional for the next generation. Moses was about to be able to wash his hands of these crazy people as he passed away, but once again, he went to bat for them.

> Then Moses said to the Lord, "O Lord, you are the God who gives breath to all creatures. Please appoint a new man as leader for the community. Give them someone who will guide them wherever they go and will lead them into battle, so the community of the Lord will not be like sheep without a shepherd."
> Numbers 27:15-17

He deeply cared for them and didn't want to see them wander aimlessly once he was gone. So the Lord called Joshua. Moses prepared Joshua to be ready to run by laying his hands on him. He passed on his mantle of leadership. He commissioned him. And he left him with a legacy of faithfulness to follow.

The Lord buried Moses after a long, unique relationship where they knew each other face to face. The reward for a life lived well isn't that you had an amazing title. It isn't that you have mounted up wealth. The reward for a life lived well is seeing the next generation following after the Lord because they can stand on your shoulders. Let's see how tall we can get.

THE GUT CHECK–WHAT ARE YOU LEAVING BEHIND?

What are you leaving behind? This isn't a morbid moment to think about your passing, but to think of what you're building. It's a natural human impulse to want to leave a mark. But what mark are we leaving?

We get the choice of how to spend our days—seeking what looks like success to the world around us, or investing in the ones coming after us. If we're going to be people who live for impact, we need to evaluate how we're showing up. Ask yourself, will your children and sphere of influence know how to walk with God because they watched you? Are you teaching compromise by your convenience? Or faithfulness by your sacrifice?

It's a very real temptation to want life to be easy. Honestly, if you're not worried about the legacy you're building, time flies and you're done. Live every day in comfort because every moment is just yours to enjoy. But there's no fulfillment there. It's naturally baked into our beings to live a life of consequence. "[God] has planted eternity in the human heart." (Ecclesiastes 3:11) We know that life is a vapor (James 4:14), but we also know that there is something that goes past this life. Through all the growing, changing, and seasons of life, we know there is something more. A purpose to be lived with intention, because God divinely directed our hearts to know it.

This is the mark of a new journey. One walked with intention. One marked with purpose. The feeling of walking in step with the Lord is unmatched, but knowing that what we do will hold weight for generations to come is next level. Take a moment to repent for the wasted time. For self-preservation and delayed obedience. Because those days are behind us. Today marks the beginning of a new kind of training. A new kind of running.

> Therefore, since we are surrounded by such a huge crowd of witnesses to the life of faith, let us strip off every weight that slows us down, especially the sin that so easily trips us up. And let us run with endurance the race God has set before us. We do this by keeping our eyes on Jesus, the champion who initiates and perfects our faith. Because of the joy awaiting him, he endured the cross, disregarding its shame. Now he is seated in the place of honor beside God's throne. Think of all the hostility he endured from sinful people; then you won't become weary and give up.
> Hebrews 12:1-3

When I think of having to run (and I do mean *having* to run because I don't enjoy it at all!) I think of how to set myself up in the best way possible. It's hard to run. It can be uncomfortable. And it just keeps going. And going. And going. You get the point. What slows you down? Well, I'm not running in sweatpants. I'm not going to wear boots. Probably not going to be sipping Diet Coke. No, we prepare to run in a way that nothing in our control holds us back. I'm going to put on shoes that are good for running. I'm going to wear clothes that aren't heavy. Make sure I have the best tunes in my ear and water to sip on. Strip off every weight that slows us down. *Especially* the sin that so easily trips us up.

What are the things you're carrying that are slowing you down? Is it past hurts? Is it unforgiveness? Have you seen a bad example of a Christ follower in the past that has tainted your view of what's possible? These are weights I've had to strip off. You might be able to sprint with a weight, but this is an endurance race. There's no room for carrying unnecessary weight. What is it for you?

Now, what are the things in your path that are going to trip you up? Is it compromise? Is it an unhealthy relationship? Is it jealousy or gossip? Just like you know that if you run on a littered path, you risk falling, we've got to put up safeguards for our lives. If you know something is a danger to you, don't take it for granted. Protect against it! Get that leaf blower out and clear the path. These can be difficult decisions to make, but we've talked about it. It's worth pruning. It's worth getting rid of the things that will so easily trip us up.

It's an intentional race we're running. And just like we're not heading out for a marathon in combat boots and blue jeans, we're not going to finish well with old habits and relationships that are weighing us down. Every step has to be intentional. Every step requires our eyes to be on Jesus. Do the work. Clear the path. Realize that this race requires determination and focus, but there's no more fulfilling mission we could dedicate our energy to.

This race is a lifelong decision. We commit to it today, then think about it every day after. Part of why I don't like to run is that I am bored the second I begin. But this race is anything but boring. Yes, we're aiming to end well. To leave a legacy. But there are so many milestones and breathtaking views along the journey that you'll never grow tired if you keep your eyes fixed on Jesus.

When we can realize that our leg of the race isn't about crossing the finish line, but passing the baton, we can run a little harder. We don't pass the baton casually. We train for it. We reach for it. And we release it with care. I will make good decisions for myself, but when I think about how a decision will affect my child, I'm much quicker to do the hard thing that's required. Doing the hard things to run well will be the reason someone thanks you for your faithfulness one day. Someone is praying for someone like you. Let that truth steady your steps today. This is not a race we run for applause. We run to hand off the baton, so the race continues long after we're gone.

Your "yes" matters not just for your life but for theirs.

EYES ON THE PRIZE

We have to keep the end in our vision, not because that's the supreme goal and moment, but because our brains naturally prioritize the present. Every moment you're in, at that moment is the most important moment. Should I say moment one more time? The point is, be where your feet are. You've probably heard that quote before. But we do have to be intentional about fully living every moment we're given. If we're *just* looking for the end result, we'll miss all of the steps that get us there. And they're worth soaking in. On the other hand, if we lose sight of the end, we're likely to forget why we're running in the first place. Moments lose their value, and vision is lost. And we know that where there is no vision, people perish. (Proverbs 29:18)

Don't you realize that in a race everyone runs, but only one person gets the prize? So run to win! All athletes are disciplined in their training. They do it to win a prize that will fade away, but we do it for an eternal prize. So I run with purpose in every step. I am not just shadowboxing. I discipline my body like an athlete, training it to do what it should. Otherwise, I fear that after preaching to others, I myself might be disqualified.
1 Corinthians 9:24-27

There will be so many around you who give up, trip, or get lost along the way. Just like an athlete trains to be better and better at their sport, we have to do the same. We can't take for granted that we've made the right decision and things will work out for us. The Bible tells us that we do have the power of self-discipline (2 Timothy 1:7), so lean into that. The truth is, every time we clear our path from all of the things that we know will trip us up, the Enemy is there to throw new ones in front of us. We have to stay diligent and alert. That's why this book isn't called "Say Yes." It's *Every* Yes because there will always be another decision in front of you, and every yes will be important.

I press on to reach the end of the race and receive the heavenly prize for which God, through Christ Jesus, is calling us.
Philippians 3:14

Live like your life is not your own, because it isn't. Eternity is watching. And so is the next generation. This is the kind of legacy worth living for. One that outlives us, honors God, and ignites faith in generations yet to come.

CONCLUSION
No More Holding Back

Let this settle in your spirit:

> God will finish what He started in me: "There has never been the slightest doubt in my mind that the God who started this great work in you would keep at it and bring it to a flourishing finish."
> Philippians 1:6 MSG

God doesn't abandon what He begins. And he hasn't abandoned you.

Before you read this book, maybe you hadn't received some of this information. Perhaps some of these challenges had not been presented to you. But now that you know, you're accountable to respond. This is your turning point. A divine interruption. It's time to do something new. This isn't a book to skim and shelve. It's a directive. A holy disruption. What is your next step? What is your next yes?

We can walk from here knowing we're not left on our own, but that God is walking with us. He has called us. He wants the best for us. When we remain close to him, we will receive guidance every step of the way. Intimacy with him is the foundation of every yes we will say. The questions start to fade when we are guided by closeness with the Father. It doesn't make things easier on the surface. It doesn't make us more sure of ourselves or immune to fear. But we are able to embrace the reality that it's not our strength, it's not in our own abilities, and it's beyond our thinking. And that's ok. We're not enough, and that's exactly the way it's supposed to be. Walking in my own strength will always breed doubt. But when we can rest on the fact that our strength comes from the Lord, we can walk in a confidence that is not our own.

> Your own ears will hear him.
>   Right behind you, a voice will say,
> "This is the way you should go,"
>   whether to the right or to the left.
> Isaiah 30:21

The key in this scripture is that the voice will be right behind you. You have to stay close. He's not going to scream at you from a distance when you've run off and done your own thing. But when we remain in him, he will remain in us. Obedience isn't always easy, but it's powerful and it is fruitful.

LET'S CLEAR THE WAY AND MOVE FORWARD

This whole book is a call to action. So let's get to work! I hope you've been working through the questions and challenges you've encountered along the way, but it's time to kick it into high gear. We're here for a purpose, and if you've made it this far into the book, then I know you're ready! There are some clear steps that a lot of us will need to take first to clear the slate. Before we can move forward, there's some mess we need to get out of the way so our vision isn't cloudy.

Reflect

What truth from this book challenged you the most?
What have you avoided saying yes to because of fear, pride, or comfort?

Repent

We are all guilty of trying to do things in our own strength or looking at the seed God has placed in our hands and hiding it away. It's time to put behind us anything that has kept us from saying yes to what God has called us to.

Refresh

After we put procrastination, half-hearted obedience, and self-reliance behind us, it's time for a fresh start! There is no room for shame here. We're going hard after the purpose God has entrusted us with, and shame comes straight from the enemy. It will sneak in from time to time, and you will have to continually call it out.

> We destroy arguments and every lofty opinion
> raised against the knowledge of God, and take
> every thought captive to obey Christ.
> 2 Corinthians 10:5

We have been given the power over the thoughts that would try to sneak in and take us out, so use it! When you are aware of the authority we're given to walk in, walk in it! You'll need it. When you begin walking in purpose and discovering more of what God has gifted you for, intrusive thoughts will start working overtime, so be ready to fight. They have no place here.

Recommit

Give God a fresh YES! We're starting a new thing, and it's time for a new commitment.

If you've forgotten what you're carrying...

If you're tired–still watering, still waiting, but worn down in the process...

If your heart came alive as you turned these pages, realizing you have something in your hand, and it's holy...

Today is the first day of a new journey. Today needs a fresh yes.

YOU'VE GOT THIS

The best way to walk this out is going to be in community. Talk it out with a small group of friends or a group at your church. It's so much easier to do the hard things when you have people walking alongside you. But don't put this book away without talking to a friend and taking a step. Begin the project that God has placed on your heart. Start a discipleship group. Reconcile with a friend. Share your testimony. Say yes to serving, leading, or giving where you've been holding back.

As you walk, focus on the daily rhythms that keep you close to God. The first yes is bold, but the daily yeses are what keep you aligned and grounded. Direction flows from devotion. Stay in the Word. Talk to the Lord. Keep your yeses in front of you. You've got this.

OFF YOU GO

The Lord is with you. I pray you do involve your community (It's SO important.), but I am with you, too. The fact that this book is in your hands means you've been prayed over. I truly believe everything written in these pages. God has a plan and a purpose laid out for you and really does want you to see it in all of its God ordained glory. It's not hidden. It's not a mystery. Get honest and do the work. The world is waiting for your yes. Your children are watching. Your community is impacted. And Heaven is cheering you on.

The pages are finished, but your story is not.
This is your moment. What will you do with it?
Say yes. Walk boldly. And don't look back.
Your yes is bigger than you think.

ACKNOWLEDGMENTS

I tend to learn lessons the hard way, and God has been so gracious with me through that. I knew that writing a book was something I wanted to do. I felt like it was a part of my story. But I had no desire to write just to check that off a list. I wanted it to mean something and truly be a leading from the Lord. As I have prayed over it for years, the time finally came when God, so gently, reminded me that there was something I had been passionate about as long as I had known him. Sometimes the things closest to you are the things you don't realize are so special. (Sound familiar?) I am eternally grateful for God handling me with such gentle hands over the years as he has refined, and refined... and refined me. We're still working on it, but I'm so thankful for all of the steps along the way.

My family has been incredible during this process. I've tried not to take over our free time with writing, but the permission was always there. The support was always there.

As with everything meaningful I have done so far, Brandon, you have always been the spark. Thank you for sparking this in me. You truly lead our home the way Christ asks. You are an amazing husband, and I love living life with you. I am so excited to see how forever turns out. Here's to the next spark.

Asher, thanks for thinking your mom is the greatest and not bouncing balls next to me while I'm writing. You are the face I see when I feel the weight of the words I've written, and I pray that we never falter so that when you stand on our shoulders, you can see farther than we ever could.

Danielle Doss, thank you for being the most lovely piece of iron I could ask for. I love being sharpened by you. The way we get to lead and disciple together is more than I could have dreamed of. I know that a covenant friendship like ours is not common, and I don't take it for granted at any moment.

Brandon Doss, you are my second favorite pastor, and I appreciate you so much. Thank you for your leadership and the way it balances with Brandon Matthews. Watching you guys hear the voice of God and stand strong in the face of so many saying something different will forever mark me. Thank you for being an encouragement and fellow leftie.

Pastor Frankie Powell, if there's one thing I know, it's that I wouldn't be where I am today without you and your leadership at World Outreach Center. That experience restored my faith in what church could be and should be. Thank you for continuing to lead me so well in all of the seasons since then. You are truly a pastor's pastor.

Cultivate Church, you have my heart. Thank you for striving to be the Church God called us to be.

For all of the prayers, encouragement, and life lessons that have happened along the way in my life so far, I am more grateful than words can say. There are so many moments that have shaped me along the way. Thank you for the hand you've had in my life.

ABOUT THE AUTHOR

Jen Matthews is a worship and creative pastor at Cultivate Church, where she serves alongside her husband, Brandon Matthews. Together, they are raising their son, Asher, with intentional faith. She co-leads *SHE*, the women's ministry of Cultivate Church, and co-hosts the *SHE Grows Podcast*, where biblical truth and real-life discipleship empower women to grow deeper in their walk with Christ. With a heart for the local church and a passion for helping others discover their calling, she lives to see people step boldly into the purpose God designed for them.

She believes your purpose is on the other side of your obedience, and every "yes" matters.

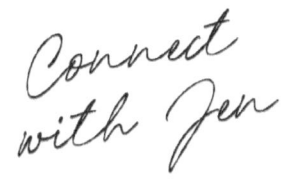

www.jenmatthews.tv
@jenkmatthews
@shegrowspodcast

Take the Journey Farther

EVERY YES

discussion guide

EVERY YES

how radical obedience unlocks your purpose.

JEN MATTHEWS

365 DAYS of purpose

the EVERY YES companion journal

JEN MATTHEWS

YOU ARE HERE

I've created a free downloadable discussion guide so you can do the work in community. It's truly the way we operate best, so grab some friends or host a small group, and let's do it together!

Ready to go hard? I have created a 356 day journal for just that purpose! It's undated so you're not held captive to being perfect with it, but each day has a scripture that will help you walk out the principles of Every Yes, as well as a thought provoking question for you to work through. Get ready for 365 days of PURPOSE!

Find the Journal and free Discussion Guide at jenmatthews.tv